The Major Themes of the Bible

by
Foster H. Shannon

GREEN LEAF PRESS

THE MAJOR THEMES OF THE BIBLE

Copyright © 1990 by Foster H. Shannon

All rights reserved. No part of this book may be reproduced in any manner whatsoever without the written permission of the publisher, except in the case of brief quotations embodied in critical articles and reviews.

ISBN 0-938462-14-8

Library of Congress Catalog Card Number: 90-081387

The Scripture quotations in this book are from the Revised Standard Version of the Bible, copyrighted 1946, 1952 © 1971, 1973 by the Division of Christian Education of the National Council of the Churches of Christ in the U.S.A., and used by permission.

GREEN LEAF PRESS, P. O. Box 6880, Alhambra, CA 91802

PRINTED IN THE UNITED STATES OF AMERICA

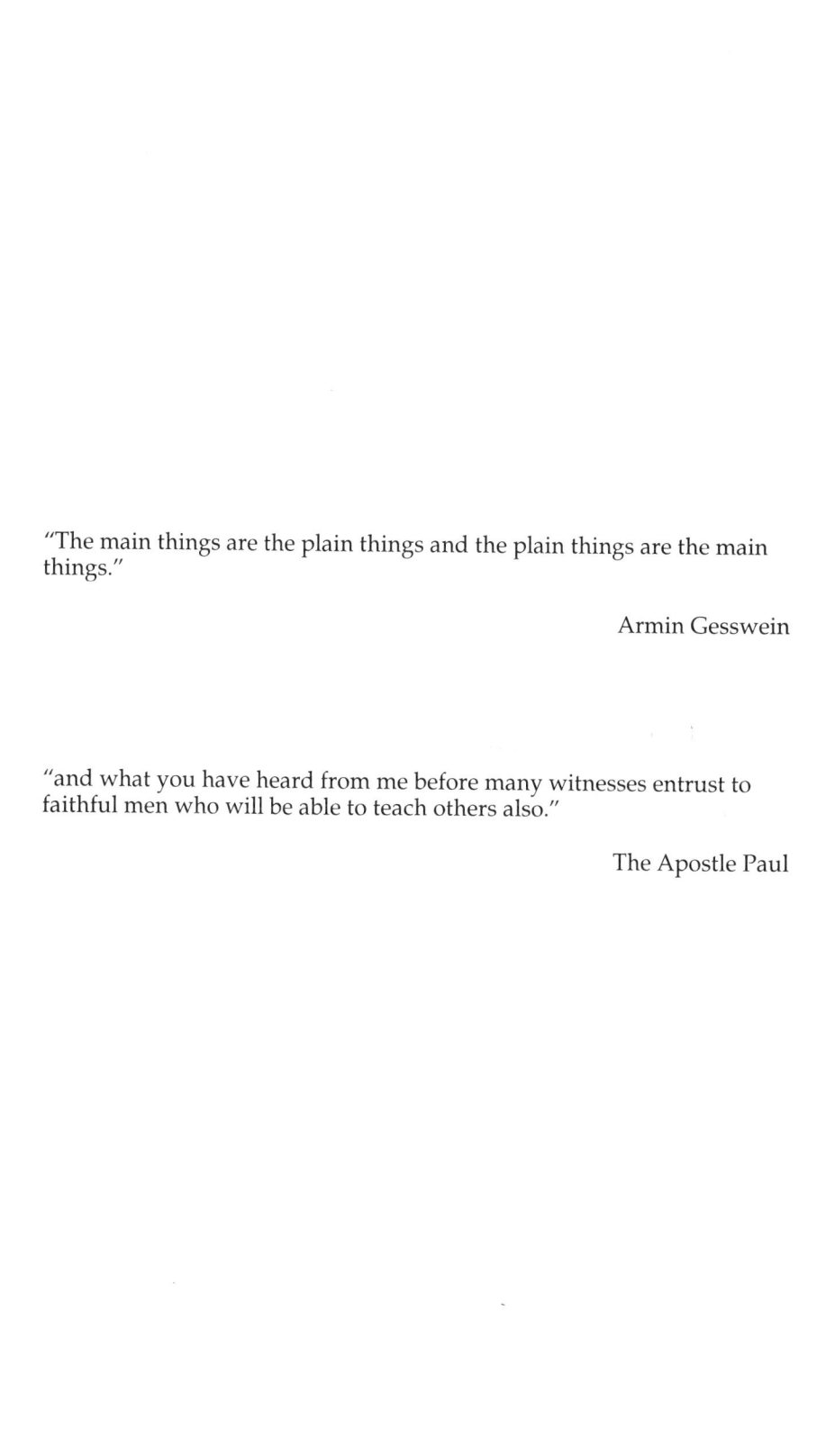

"The main things are the plain things and the plain things are the main things."

Armin Gesswein

"and what you have heard from me before many witnesses entrust to faithful men who will be able to teach others also."

The Apostle Paul

THE MAJOR THEMES OF THE BIBLE

INTRODUCTION		vii
CHAPTER ONE	THE INSPIRATION AND AUTHORITY OF SCRIPTURE	1
CHAPTER TWO	THE GREATNESS OF GOD	12
CHAPTER THREE	THE LOVE OF GOD	21
CHAPTER FOUR	THE PROBLEM OF SIN	31
CHAPTER FIVE	THE DEVIL AND THE POWERS OF EVIL	40
CHAPTER SIX	DIVINE JUDGMENT	51
CHAPTER SEVEN	SALVATION IN JESUS CHRIST	63
CHAPTER EIGHT	THE RESURRECTION OF JESUS CHRIST	73
CHAPTER NINE	THE HOLY SPIRIT	85
CHAPTER TEN	PRAYER	97
CHAPTER ELEVEN	THE KINGDOM OF GOD	107
CHAPTER TWELVE	THE AUTHORITY OF JESUS CHRIST	115
CHAPTER THIRTEEN	THE CHURCH	127
CHAPTER FOURTEEN	THE BLESSINGS OF THE NEW COVENANT	135
CHAPTER FIFTEEN	NEW LIFE AND SPIRITUAL GROWTH	147
CHAPTER SIXTEEN	EVANGELISM AND WORLD MISSION	156
CHAPTER SEVENTEEN	PRINCIPLES OF JUSTICE AND COMPASSION	166

CHAPTER EIGHTEEN	THE RETURN OF CHRIST AND ENSUING EVENTS	178
CHAPTER NINETEEN	HEAVEN AND ETERNAL LIFE	187
APPENDICES	Selected Biblical Passages on the Divine Nature of Jesus Christ	197
INDEX		201

INTRODUCTION

The Bible is the greatest book in the world. It is profound. One can spend a lifetime in its study and, in a sense, never master it. There is always more to be learned, contemplated and integrated into one's thinking. However thorough one's study of the Bible, there are always substantial areas that remain to be investigated.

Having said the above—many of the truths of the Bible are as plain as day. One must go to great lengths to avoid or to distort them: That God was before all things, that he is the creator of all, that every person has sinned and rightfully come under the judgment of God, that God choose a particular nation for himself under the Old Covenant. That it is God's passionate purpose to reconcile multitudes to himself through his Son, Jesus Christ; that Christ fully atoned for the sins of those who believe in him through his sacrifice upon the cross. That Christ established the church to make the good news of his salvation known, that he has ascended to heaven, is with God the Father, and will one day return to earth, fully establish his kingdom, and bring the consummation of all things. These aforementioned truths from scripture illustrate the clarity of much that the Bible affirms.

The purpose of this book is not to deal with what is obscure, novel, previously unrevealed, concealed, hidden, or peripheral. Our quest is for what is central and vital. What are the major themes of the Bible? That is—what are those doctrines, truths, or commands that are strongly emphasized in the whole of the Bible; those truths that receive an extraordinary emphasis? I believe, with the majority of Christians throughout history, that the Bible is the word of God; that it is true in whole and in part—and that it is the final authority for those who believe in God.

Because it is such a great and profound book, one cannot have every part of the Bible in his or her consciousness at any given moment. Therefore, it is important to recognize those truths that are relatively more significant. There is a main current of scripture, from Genesis through Revelation, that flows more swiftly and is more easily discerned—while the river of biblical revelation is itself broader with many pools and eddies and even some muddy spots along the banks!

Part of Jesus' quarrel with the Pharisees was that they could not tell the forest from the trees. They elevated relatively lesser doctrines to positions of greater importance, and failed to acknowledge many of the major truths of the Old Covenant:

> Woe to you, scribes and Pharisees, hypocrites! for you tithe mint and dill and cummin, and have neglected the weightier matters of the law, justice and mercy and faith; these you ought to have done, without neglecting the others. You blind guides, straining out a gnat and swallowing a camel! [Matthew 23:23,24]

Jesus did not hesitate to point out the relative superiority of certain biblical truths:

> And one of them, a lawyer, asked him a question to test him. Teacher, which is the great commandment in the law? And he said to him, You shall love the Lord your God with all your heart, and with all your soul, and with all your mind. This is the great and first commandment. And a second is like it, You shall love your neighbor as yourself. On these two commandments depend all the law and the prophets. [Matthew 22:35-40]

A number of Old Testament passages emphasize that certain matters are especially central:

> He has showed you, O man, what is good; and what does the Lord require of you but to do justice, and to love kindness, and to walk humbly with your God? [Micah 6:8]

> Hear, O Israel: The Lord our God is one Lord; and you shall love the Lord your God with all your heart, and with all your soul, and with all your might. [Deuteronomy 6:4,5]

> The end of the matter; all has been heard. Fear God, and keep his commandments; for this is the whole duty of man. [Ecclesiastes 12:13]

New Testament passages also point clearly to a body of doctrine that is at the heart of Christian belief:

> ... and what you have heard from me before many witnesses entrust to faithful men who will be able to teach others also. [II Timothy 2:2]

> Therefore let us leave the elementary doctrine of Christ and go on to maturity,... [Hebrews 6:1]

> ... he [a bishop] must hold firm to the sure word as taught, so that he may be able to give instruction in sound doctrine and also to confute those who contradict it. [Titus 1:9]

This attempt to state the major themes of the Bible is essentially the product of biblical theology rather than of systematic theology. Systematic theology seeks to derive a logical system of doctrine from scripture (sometimes to impose a structure upon scripture!). The logical development of thought from the Bible is important and has been developed in many writings. The weakness of the "systematic" approach is that it may ignore important matters, which do not conform to its logical system, or it may render a major theme in the Bible to a sub-point in its structure.

The study of the Bible should, ordinarily, be inductive rather than deductive. It is, of course, quite proper to seek additional support from scripture for those doctrines that have been derived from it! Both systematic theology and biblical theology should be inductive, but I think that biblical theology, which follows the stream or flow of scripture from beginning to end is more likely to be inductive. Having said this much, it must be recognized that the two approaches inevitably overlap. Both make valuable contributions to biblical understanding.

Attempts to set forth the major themes of scripture are relatively rare when compared to systematic or doctrinal works on the Bible. This book is intended primarily for the lay person rather than for the specialist. It will, I hope, be found to be clear and readable. I believe that it can also contribute to a continuing conversation about the Bible. Everything in scripture is important and everything is to be received, but some matters are of more weight than others. I will look forward to those comments or suggestions of what should have been included, that has not been, or of what should have been more fully developed. Yes, even comments on what has been given more attention than it deserved (given the intent of this work)!

How, then, do we discern the major themes of scripture? What is to determine those matters that are of greater weight and those matters that are of lesser weight? Here are six principles that I have followed. This is not to say that each of the themes are supported by all six principles. Many are. But if not all six—the others have been informed by most of them.

1. It is a theme common to both the Old Testament and the New Testament.

2. It is repeated many times in a number of books of the Bible.

3. It was very important to Jesus and/or central to his teaching.

4. It is a foundational truth upon which other important truths of the Bible rest.

5. It is emphasized in the book of Acts.

[The book of Acts is especially important from a hermeneutical (interpretive) perspective, because it is our best indicator of how the apostles and the early church understood the words of Jesus. The Roman Catholic Church could have avoided a number of important deviations from the mainstream of Christianity had it given more careful attention to the hermeneutical significance of the book of Acts.]

6. Is it a truth emphasized in those parts of scripture that by their character or placement emphasize importance? e.g. the opening and closing chapters of the Bible; the final words of Jesus; concluding summaries of the apostle Paul; those parts of scripture that are more deliberately didactic, e.g. Matthew 5-7; Matthew 23

and 24; John 7-10; John 14-16, and especially the books of Romans, Galatians, Ephesians, and Colossians and the summaries of the book of Hebrews.

I hope that this book will assist many in fulfilling important commissions of the Bible:

> Do your best to present yourself to God as one approved, a workman who has no need to be ashamed, rightly handling the word of truth. [II Timothy 2:15]

> All scripture is inspired by God and profitable for teaching, for reproof, for correction, and for training in righteousness, that the man of God may be complete, equipped for every good work. [II Timothy 3:16,17]

CHAPTER ONE

THE INSPIRATION AND AUTHORITY OF SCRIPTURE

The Bible is the key to the Christian faith, to our understanding of Jesus Christ, and our belief in him. Without the Bible, we would know little or nothing of Jesus and very little of God's purposes and intentions for us. Nor, would we be clear on how we are to be saved, that is, how people are to have a right relationship with God. The believability and the reliability of the scriptures is an important issue both within and without the Christian community. The Bible has to do with whether or not God has spoken in such a way that he may be believed and trusted.

There is another way to approach it. The Bible has to do with the authority of God over people's lives. If a person recognizes the scriptures to be true, reliable and authoritative, then he or she may have a high regard for what the scriptures say. If one has serious qualms, serious doubts, serious questions about the reliability of the scriptures--then he will not likely be under the authority of Jesus Christ. We cannot have a Bible of dubious reliability and an authoritative Christ. To undermine the authority of the scriptures is to restrict or reject the authority of Christ.

One thing can be said, at the outset, in considering the theme of "The Inspiration and Authority of Scripture": Any of the standard translations of the Bible are quite adequate. One can be assured that he has a reliable English language text whether one uses the King James Version, the American Standard Version, the Revised Standard Version, the New English Bible, or the New International Version. The text of any of those versions adequately conveys what the writers of the biblical books originally wrote. One can be more certain about the accuracy and the adequacy of the biblical text than of any other ancient writing.

The Bible is like Ivory Soap. It is 99 and 44/100% pure! It is true that there are minor discrepancies in the best Hebrew and Greek manuscripts of the books of the Bible, but they are not significant. To avoid even minor discrepancies, God would have to perform a miracle every time a person wrote down a passage from the Bible. In other words, if the biblical text were to be absolutely free from transmissional errors--it would require that if one would sit down to copy a page out of the Bible--God would have to guarantee, that in every instance of such copying, absolutely no mistakes would be allowed. God has not chosen to preserve the scriptures in that way. What he has done is to give us a treasury of manuscripts that are very close to the originals.

When compared and weighed against each other, the relatively minor errors in the manuscripts begin to cancel one another out and lead us very close to the original text. Taken together, the best manuscripts perform the function of a powerful magnifying glass. They bring a text into view that for all intents and purposes is identical to the original text. The discovery of the Isaiah manuscript in one of the Qumran caves in 1947 substantiated our confidence in the accuracy of the biblical manuscripts. Although it was four or five hundred years older than the previous earliest Isaiah manuscript, there were no substantial differences between that text and previously accepted Hebrew texts of Isaiah.

The Bible is the word of God. It is true. And truth can stand the light. There are some plants that thrive in the sunlight. There are other plants that must be carefully sheltered. If they are exposed to direct sunlight they will wither and die. The Bible is not like one of those plants that need careful protection. It is sturdy truth, and can always stand up to honest examination.

We must also recognize that as we consider the sixty-six books of the Bible (thirty-nine books of the Old Testament and twenty-seven books of the New Testament) that it is bigger than any one of us. No one will wholly and completely master the full text of the scriptures. We should be studying the Bible everyday. We should be growing in our knowledge of the scriptures. And by God's grace, by means of his Holy Spirit, as we study his word he will change and reform our lives. We call this the process of sanctification, spiritual growth. But as faithfully and as assiduously as any person studies the Bible, he or she will not have completely mastered the Bible. There will always be areas in which one's understanding of scripture is incomplete. There will always be parts of the Bible that demand further examination. It is appropriate to approach the scriptures with a good portion of humility regarding one's capacities for analysis and understanding.

The Bible claims for itself to be the inspired and authoritative word of God. A person may believe it to be the word of God or he may choose to believe that it is not. But there should be no question that the Bible makes this claim for itself. II Timothy 3:16 states, "All scripture is inspired by God and profitable for teaching, for reproof, for correction, and for training in righteousness." The entire Bible is inspired by God. Jesus, on many occasions, endorsed the thirty-nine books of the Old Testament as the very word of God. For example, Matthew 5:17,18,

> Think not that I have come to abolish the law and the prophets; I have come not to abolish them but to fulfil them. For truly, I say to you, till heaven and earth pass away, not an iota, not a dot, will pass from the law until all is accomplished.

In a few instances, Jesus modified certain Old Testament teachings by virtue of his divine authority. For example, Mark 7:18,19 tells us that Jesus declared all foods to be clean, signifying that the time for the keeping of the Old Testament rules regarding clean and unclean meats had come to an end. But Jesus, by his own word, upholds the Old Testament scriptures. He held them to be the very word of God, which must be observed--which will be fulfilled--and which will assuredly be fully accomplished.

The Bible is replete with statements that it is the word of God. We read in Matthew 11:10, "This is he of whom it is written,...". In other words, in presenting Jesus Christ Matthew called upon the Old Testament saying, in effect, we can believe in Jesus Christ as the Messiah of God because the authoritative word of God spoke of him. Matthew 12:17 states, "This was to fulfill what was spoken by the prophet Isaiah:". The words of Isaiah (being the word of God) are now being fulfilled. A similar formula is used in Matthew 13:14, "With them indeed is fulfilled the prophecy of Isaiah...". Here again the Old Testament is referred to as the true word of God being fulfilled in the life and ministry of Jesus. II Peter 1:20,21 states,

> First of all you must understand this, that no prophecy of

scripture is a matter of one's own interpretation, because no prophecy ever came by the impulse of man, but men moved by the Holy Spirit spoke from God.

More than three hundred times in the Old and New Testaments the claim is made that these words are the very word of God. In addition to those more than three hundred direct claims--the inferential references and assumptions in the scriptures that this is, indeed, the inspired word of God bring such affirmations in the Bible into the thousands. In the Greek text of the New Testament the word, grafe is found approximately fifty times. Grafe means, "it is written", and it always means or implies inspired; that is God-inspired scripture. The Bible clearly claims to be the very word of God.

The Bible also has been recognized to be inspired and authoritative by the believing community. When we study the sermons, lessons, lectures, commentaries, and writings of those who are within the Christian community from the second century to the present--by far the great majority use the scriptures in that sense. That is, that the scriptures are the authoritative word of God. When we consult the great historic creeds and confessions of the church, both in their direct and inferential statements--they unequivocally hold to a high view of the scriptures as the very word of God.

Within the context of the Christian community--there are only three possible ways to relate to the scriptures. The first is that of the mediaeval church up until the time of the Reformation: that the church itself is the infallible, authoritative interpreter of scripture. That view has some appeal. The collective wisdom of the Christian community for 1900 years is not to be lightly regarded! When we read the Bible, and consider what it means, we certainly should have regard for what other Christians have understood it to mean. And this must necessarily include what important segments of the church have stated it to mean. But the problem with this point of view (in making the church the interpreter of the Bible) is that the authority is shifted from the Bible to the church. The Reformers knew that peril first hand and sought to reaffirm the unique authority of scripture.

Second: Individualism has been a chronic characteristic of the twentieth century. The result is to make some individual the authoritative interpreter of scripture. (For some Protestants scholarly authority has replaced the Pope.) In the final analysis, it is up to each person individually to understand what the Bible means, and to faithfully live by it in the light of that understanding. But that is not exactly what I am saying. I am saying that to make an individual Christian or a minister or a Christian leader the final interpreter of scripture for others is a serious mistake. And the scriptures themselves remind us of that. We should certainly hope that we have scholars and preachers who can help us understand the Bible. We believe that the insights of many Christians can contribute to our own understanding of scripture. But that is quite different from making an individual, however personally appealing or academically qualified, the final authority on what the scriptures say.

The third view is that the scriptures are themselves authoritative, and in the final analysis are their own interpreter. This was the view of Luther, Zwingli, and John Calvin. I believe that this is the correct view of the Bible. It is not proper to transfer the authority of the Bible to the church.

> But there has very generally prevailed a most pernicious error, that the Scriptures have only so much weight as is conceded to them by the suffrages of the Church;... It is a very false notion, therefore, that the power of judging of the Scripture belongs to the Church, so as to make the certainty of it dependent on the Church's will. [John Calvin, Institutes of the Christian Religion, Book I, Chapter VII]

Nor can we convey the authority of the Bible to some convincing, charasmatic, or authoritative individual. That authority resides in the Bible itself. This principle is illustrated in Acts 17:11. The apostle Paul was on his second missionary journey. He had been in Philippi and Thessalonica in Macedonia, and as he traveled southward toward Athens and Corinth he arrived in Beroea. We read the following marvelous statement in Acts 17:11,

> Now these Jews were more noble than those in Thessalonica, for they received the word with all eager-

ness, examining the scriptures daily to see if these things were so.

Here was the great apostle Paul coming to deliver the gospel of Jesus Christ to the people in Beroea, and these people studied the Old Testament scriptures to make sure that Paul was speaking accurately. If it was appropriate to check up on Paul's fidelity to scripture, anyone who claims to represent the Bible should be pleased to have his statements compared with what the scriptures actually say. The scriptures contain their own authority, and that authority must not be usurped.

The Bible does present certain difficulties to the modern mind. For instance, the Genesis account of the creation, of the origin of the world, of life on earth, of the origin of the human race, and of the flood seem to some to be disharmonious with contemporary scientific concepts. I deal more comprehensively with such questions in my book, *God Is Light*. This apparent conflict should be taken seriously. It is vitally important to discern between the philosophical structures that are erected on the foundation of scientific fact, and to understand that there is a qualitative difference between the foundation of fact and the superstructure of theory erected upon that fact. When the biblical text is carefully read for what it actually says and then compared with empirical data rather than with current opinion (no matter how widely held) the difficulties are, at the very least, reduced to manageable proportions.

If one carefully reads what the Bible says about origins and compares that with fully established scientific facts there is no significant conflict. The conflict arises between what the Bible is perceived to say, on the one hand, and scientific hypothesis and theory on the other. If we will take, what we assuredly know through science and (avoid confusing theory with fact), and then relate that fact as precisely as possible to what the Bible says-- there will not be any substantial difficulties or problems. Most such problems result from the contrast between the philosophical schemes that people construct from scientific fact and unwarranted assumptions that Christians sometimes make. If, for example, one believes that the creation was accomplished by God in six consecutive twenty-four hour days that is his right and privilege. But that is not a necessary reading of the biblical text. That particular point of view is substantially out of harmony with the scientific fact of an Earth that is more than four billion years old and of a universe that is, perhaps, fifteen billion years old. Well meaning Christians can impose unnecessary structures on the Bible, just as others can raise unnecessary and false juxtapositions between the Bible and science.

There are those who believe that the Bible contradicts itself in significant areas--and because it contradicts itself, it is not to be believed. If one were to take all of the perceived contradictions in the Bible--put them in a kettle and bring them to the boiling point--the insignificant ones would evaporate. The residue would be less than a teacup of serious problems. The remaining problems can be handled in several ways. As we have acknowledged, there are minor textual errors in the Bible. Some humility in this area is appropriate. It is appropriate to recognize that in our approach to the Bible we may not be quite as clever or as knowledgeable as we think we are. Some of the apparent intellectual problems related to the Bible may derive from defective transmission between the original text and a contemporary text in current use--not from statements that were inherent in the original text.

It should be recognized that the scriptures deal with the great themes of life as no other writing does. Certain of these themes are held in a dialectical tension in the Bible. For example, the immanence of God (God's nearness--God's presence) and the transcendence of God (God's otherness, the mystery of God, God's holiness). How does a single human mind master such truths: the presence of God, the nearness of God, the immanence of God and the transcendence or otherness of God? There is a dialectical tensions between salvation by faith alone and the importance of works on the part of the Christian. This is a tension within the scriptures because they present some truths that are very difficult for our minds to grasp simultaneously. However, we are not dealing with essential contradiction. It is simply that there is more there than any individual can embrace. We acknowledge, then, some difficulties in the Bible. But, I believe, the person who is honest in his inquiry will find more than sufficient answers to those difficulties. The other side of the story is that much of the Bible commends itself to us in a most convincing way.

If God does not exist, creation and life and everything in our awareness is a mystery at best and an absurdity at worst. If God exists, and human beings are the work of his creative activity, it is reasonable to suppose that he has communicated with his creatures in some way. If the Bible is not true--if the Bible is not the Word of God--if God has not communicated to us in and through the writers of scripture, then it is highly unlikely that he has communicated with the human race by some other means. If the Bible fails the test, it is extremely unlikely that any other religious writing or system will be found acceptable!

Indeed, as we examine the scriptures we must marvel at them. The thirty-nine books of the Old Testament and the twenty-seven books of the New Testament cannot be assessed as simply a product of their times. That is, they cannot be adequately explained as an appropriate or natural product of the culture of which they were a part. When we study the cultural milieu from which the various books of the Bible derived--we should conclude that they are, indeed, the work of God!

There are at least eight major philosophical and religious systems or world-views: Hedonism (of which Playboy Magazine is a notable exponent), Materialism (of which Marxism is one of the most significant branches), Nihilism (life is a farce, or an enigma, or not worth living--or all three), Scientism, Islam, Bhuddism, Hinduism, Animism, and Christianity. Of these eight-- Christianity, Marxism, and Scientism (scientific humanism) are the heavyweight contenders. The Bible presents a thoroughgoing world-view and understanding of life. In the gospel of John, chapter six, many people had ceased following Jesus because of the high demands of his teachings. In response to this dismaying withdrawal Jesus inquired of his disciples, "Will you also go away?". Simon Peter responded, "Lord, to whom shall we go? You have the words of eternal life;" Our minds may throw roadblocks in the way of finding a theoretical absolute pure infallible truth--but they remain capable of apprehending the best truth.

When compared to other world systems, the scriptures distinguish themselves. On the whole, Christians are happier than those who are not Christians. This is evidenced in thousands upon thousands of personal testimonies. It is been verified by the Gallup organization. Indeed, those Christians who most carefully follow the precepts of scripture are the happiest of all.

> A total of 44% of the national adult population say they are "very happy", while 51% say "fairly" and 5% "not too happy."
> The highest proportion of those in the "very happy" category are persons who are highly spiritually committed, with 68% offering this self-assessment.
> Also high in terms of those saying they are very happy are persons who attend church more than weekly, those who feel they are living "very Christian lives," members of evangelical churches, and those who place themselves on the far right in terms of their religious beliefs.
> Those in low religiosity categories are far less likely to say they are "very happy." For example, only 29% of those who feel they are living "a not very Christian life" indicate this high level of happiness.
> [Emerging Trends, Dec., 1982, p. 4]

The biblical assessment of human nature is the most realistic. It avoids the pessimism of a Bhuddism that literally denies the value of this life in seeking release from it. It also avoids the foolish optimism of Marxism and of many of the advocates of scientific humanism who contend that either time or institutional and societal adjustments will solve all of the problems of the human race. The scriptures correctly identify the human problem as essentially one of relationship. The created need to be in proper harmonious relationship with their creator. That means that God's creatures must repent of their sins and believe in God and obey him.

> The earth is the Lord's and the fullness thereof, the world and those who dwell therein; for he has founded it upon the seas, and established it upon the rivers. Who shall ascend the hill of the Lord? And who shall stand in his holy place? He who has clean hands and a pure heart, who does not lift up his soul to what is false, and does not swear deceitfully. [Psalm 24:1-4]

The only telling complaints registered against the morality and ethics found in the Bible is that they are too exacting--too high-- indeed at times unachievable. But where do we go to find a superior moral/ethical system? The words of Edmund Burke are apt,

> "The writers against religion, whilst they oppose every system, are wisely careful never to set up any of their own."

It is difficult to improve on the words of the Psalmist:

> The law of the Lord is perfect, reviving the soul; the testimony of the Lord is sure, making wise the simple, the precepts of the Lord are right, rejoicing the heart; the commandment of the Lord is pure, enlightening the eyes; the fear of the Lord is clean, enduring for ever; the ordinances of the Lord are true, and righteous altogether. More to be desired are they than gold, even much fine gold; sweeter also than honey and drippings of the honeycomb.
> [Psalm 19:7-10]

Further Reading

Beegle, Dewey M. *God's Word Into English,* Harper & Brothers, 1960.

The Book of Confessions, Office of the General Assembly, Presbyterian Church, (U.S.A.)

Bruce, F.F., *The New Testament Documents: Are They Reliable?,* Inter Varsity Press, 1975.

Lewis, C.S., *Miracles*

Lockyer, Herbert, *All The Doctrines of the Bible,* Preface and Chapters I, II, and III.

Rogers, Jack, *Presbyterian Creeds,* The Westminster Press, 1985.

For Reflection or Discussion

1. If, indeed, God can be known--what are some possible ways that he might make himself known to people? Which way would be the best?

2. What was Jesus' attitude toward the Old Testament scriptures?

3. What are some problems associated with believing that the Bible is the very word of God? What are some problems associated with rejecting that belief?

4. List four or five "problems" or "contradictions" associated with the Bible. What answers or resolutions can you give to these problems?

CHAPTER TWO

THE GREATNESS OF GOD

The greatness of God was caught by many persons who encountered him, as related by the Bible. And I believe it is meant for us to share their experiences as we read the pages of scripture. Moses was in the Sinai area watching over his sheep. He saw a bush that was burning. Yet it was not consumed by the fire, and he drew near to see what was happening. God spoke to him out of the bush saying,

> Do not come near; put off your shoes from your feet, for the place on which you are standing is holy ground. And he said, I am the God of your father, the God of Abraham, the God of Isaac, and the God of Jacob. [Exodus 3:5,6]

Moses hid his face, for he was afraid to look at God. As his awareness of the greatness of God was heightened--he sensed his own unholiness and unworthiness.

Job was blessed by God as few people have been. He was cited by God as one of the most exemplary individuals who have ever lived. Yet, for a time, God allowed Job to be given over to the power of Satan. He suffered the loss of his family, of his possessions, his health, and even his respectability. As anyone would do, Job questioned all that had befallen him. He reached for answers that were beyond his grasp. Then God revealed to Job more of his glory and greatness. Job comprehended the grandeur of God as he had not before. Here is what we read near the end of the book of Job,

> Then Job answered the Lord: "I know that thou canst do all things, and that no purpose of thine can be thwarted. Who is this that hides counsel without knowledge? Therefore I have uttered what I did not understand, things too wonderful for me, which I did not know. Hear, and I will speak; I will question you, and you declare to me. I had heard of thee by the hearing of the ear, but now my eye sees thee; therefore I despise myself, and repent in dust and ashes." [Job 42:1-6]

The Greatness of God

Moses encountered God, and he was afraid even to look at God. Job suffered greatly--perhaps more than any person other than our Lord Jesus Christ. And Job asked why? He questioned God. God revealed himself more fully to Job, and Job repented because of the great distance between himself and God.

In the sixth chapter of Isaiah, as God called Isaiah into ministry, we read of the marvelous experiences of the prophet as he realized the exaltation of God.

> In the year that King Uzziah died I saw the Lord sitting upon a throne, high and lifted up; and his train filled the temple. Above him stood the seraphim; each had six wings: with two he covered his face, and with two he covered his feet, and with two he flew. And one called to another and said: Holy, holy, holy is the Lord of hosts; the whole earth is full of his glory. And the foundations of the thresholds shook at the voice of him who called, and the house was filled with smoke. And I said: Woe is me! For I am lost; for I am a man of unclean lips; for my eyes have seen the King, the Lord of hosts!   [Isaiah 6:1-5]

Isaiah had a vision of God, and it humbled him. The prophet Habakkuk wrote, " ... the Lord is in his holy temple; let all the earth keep silence before him."

Early in the ministry of Jesus there is an incident that may appear to be of less significance than these visions and revelations to Moses and Job and Isaiah. Probably before Jesus had issued a formal call to the twelve to be his apostles, Jesus was in a fishing boat with Peter, James, John, and others. These men were engaged in the business of fishing on the Sea of Galilee. They had labored all night, casting their nets many times, and had caught nothing. Jesus told them to put out into the deep and to try again. We read that there was such a great catch of fish that their nets were breaking, and they had to bring a second boat out to help them handle that tremendous haul of fish. Peter's response was not so much over the great bonanza they had received, nor over the money he would realize from the sale of the fish. He was amazed at the tremendous miracle that had occurred. We read of his response in Luke 5:8, "But when Simon Peter saw it, he fell down at Jesus' knees, saying, 'Depart from me, for I am a sinful man, O Lord.'" Peter saw God at work, and seeing God at work made Peter aware of the presence of God. And the presence of God made him aware of the greatness and of the holiness of God—and of his own inadequacy.

The primary way that the greatness of God is illustrated and celebrated in scripture is in a contemplation of his creative works. God has made everything that is. The vast universe, our solar system, and the planet on which we live are all the handiwork of God. God has made both the animate and the inanimate; plant life and animal life and man, himself. The Bible states that people are created in the very image of God. The Bible begins in Genesis, chapter one, affirming that God is the Creator. And the clear implication, all the way through the Bible, is that if, indeed, he is the Creator--if, indeed, he has made all that is, then he is the source of all power and all authority. He alone is worthy of worship, and it is imperative that he be worshipped and honored as God.

> The heavens are thine, the earth also is thine; the world and all that is in it, thou hast founded them. The north and the south, thou hast created them; [Psalm 89:11,12]

God's greatness is demonstrated in his creative power. In Psalm 19 we read, "The heavens are telling the glory of God; and the firmament proclaims his handiwork." One of the advantages of living in the twentieth century is that we have the opportunity of appreciating the greatness of the universe to a degree that people of former generations could not. As far as we can ascertain, the universe extends outward from us in all directions for more than ten billion light years. That greatly exceeds the limits of our comprehension! We understand that light travels at 186,000 miles per second. Our best understanding is that the light or radio waves from the most distant known objects in the universe have taken more than ten billion light years to reach us! An awareness of such a vast realm and the incredible distances in the universe should surely cause one to marvel at the great work that God has done.

> Of old thou didst lay the foundation of the earth, and the heavens are the work of thy hands. They will perish, but thou dost endure; they will all wear out like a garment.

Thou changest them like raiment, and they pass away; but thou art the same, and thy years have no end.
[Psalm 102:25-27]

God has created all of the stars including the Sun around which our planet orbits. The Sun is approximately 865,000 miles in diameter. However, some stars have a diameter that is 800 times that of the Sun. For example, the star, Antares, is 173 million miles in diameter! To help in comprehending its immensity—if one would begin at the center of the Sun and move out to the orbit of Mercury—and then Venus—and then Earth—and then Mars—Antares would more than fill that immense space. It is that large. Beatelguese is even larger at 190 million miles in diameter, and Alpha Hercules is over 500 million miles in diameter. Again, using the analogy of our solar system. Put Alpha Hercules in the center, and it would fill all of the space in our solar system to a greater extent that the orbit of the planet Jupiter!

The estimates of the number of stars in the Milky Way, our own galaxy, vary. I gather no one has counted them! The Milky Way is what one sees on a clear cloudless night when there is no moon and one views a beautiful glowing haze above in the sky. That glowing haze is composed of millions and millions of stars. Most estimates are that there are more than 100 million stars in the Milky Way. Some estimate several hundreds of millions of stars in that one galaxy. Now the Milky Way is only one galaxy, and we are told that there are possibly 100 billion galaxies. The heavens, indeed, declare the glory of God!

The apostle Paul, reflecting on the creative work of God, wrote to the church in Rome,

> For what can be known about God is plain to them, because God has shown it to them. Ever since the creation of the world his invisible nature, namely, his eternal power and deity, has been clearly perceived in the things that have been made. [Romans 1:19,20]

He is saying that if we consider--meditate on--think about the world, the solar system, the universe, we must surely recognize that there is a Creator, and that he is a God of enormous power.

The greatness of God is even more clearly understood through those further things that the scriptures teach us of him. The Bible declares that God is eternal--that he is unique. There is an absolute difference between an infinite God and the finite people whom he has made. People are created by God. They have a beginning. God is neither created or made. He always is. Moses, before the bush, inquired of God as God commissioned him to go to Egypt and represent him before Pharaoh and before his own people.

> Then Moses said to God, "If I come to the people of Israel and say to them, 'The God of your fathers has sent me to you,' and they ask me, 'What is his name?' what shall I say to them? God said to Moses, I am who I am." And he said, "Say this to the people of Israel, 'I am has sent me to you.'" [Exodus 3:13,14]

In that declaration of himself, God affirmed his eternity to Moses. He is the Alpha and the Omega; the beginning and the end. God is eternal.

God is all powerful. He is omnipotent. Isaiah proclaimed,

> "The Lord of hosts has sworn; As I have planned, so shall it be. And as I have purposed, so shall it stand." [Isaiah 14:24]

The will of God and the act of God are virtually the same thing. What God desires to do he can do. Indeed, Psalm 115:3, states "He does whatever he pleases:". Isaiah wrote,

> "For the Lord of hosts has purposed, and who will annul it? His hand is stretched out, and who will turn it back?" [Isaiah 14:27]

God possesses all knowledge. He is ominiscient. Hebrews 4:13 states, "And before him no creature is hidden, but all are open and laid bare to the eyes of him with whom we have to do." Psalm 139 wonderfully describes the omniscience and the omnipresence of God:

Psalm 139 wonderfully describes the omniscience and the omnipresence of God:

> O Lord, thou hast searched me and known me! Thou knowest when I sit down and when I rise up; thou discernest my thoughts from afar. Thou searchest out my path and my lying down, and art acquainted with all my ways. [Psalm 139:1-3]

God has total knowledge. He knows all things. Wherever one goes, God is there. The apostle Paul affirmed these truths to a group of intellectual Greeks in Athens. He said of God, "Yet he is not far from each one of us, for 'In him we live and move and have our being'." [Acts 17:28] The Psalmist wrote,

> Whither shall I go from thy Spirit? Or whither shall I flee from thy presence? If I ascend to heaven, thou art there! If I take the wings of the morning and dwell in the uttermost parts of the sea, even there thy hand shall lead me, and thy right hand shall hold me. If I say, Let only darkness cover me, and the light about me be night, even the darkness is not dark to thee, the night is bright as the day; for darkness is as light with thee. [Psalm 139:7-12]

The scriptures plainly teach that God is eternal. He is all powerful. He is all knowing. He is present everywhere.

The greatness of God is demonstrated in his mighty works of deliverance. Especially in the Psalms and in the prophets the grand and tremendous works of God are celebrated. He judged the ancient world in an awesome flood, having previously warned that world through Noah. He condemned Sodom and Gomorrah for their wickedness, raining fire and brimstone on those cities. He judged Pharaoh and the people of Egypt with ten terrible plagues for their stubbornness--for their irreconciliability--for their unwillingness to turn and to respond to him in spite of the many manifestations of his power that they had witnessed.

After the descendants of Abraham had been in Egypt for a period of 400 years and had been impressed into slavery by the armies of Egypt were engulfed in those waters.

> In the sight of their fathers he wrought marvels in the land of Egypt, in the fields of Zoan. He divided the sea and let them pass through it, and made the waters stand like a heap. In the daytime he led them with a cloud, and all the night with a fiery light. He cleft rocks in the wilderness, and gave them drink abundantly as from the deep. He made streams come out of the rock, and caused waters to flow down like rivers. [Psalm 78:12-26]

God made miraculous provisions for the people of Israel. He gave them manna six days a week for the forty years they were in the wilderness. He provided water for them, and at times gave them tremendous quantities of meat. They knew that God had been with them, and successive generations were to remember-- that they might not forget the greatness of God.

Elijah, one of God's prophets to the northern kingdom of Israel, challenged the prophets of Baal to demonstrate the power of their god, and he assured them that he could demonstrate the power of the only true God. On Mount Carmel the 450 prophets of Baal prepared their sacrifice. They called on Baal, they cried out, and cut themselves, "but there was no voice, no one answered, no one heeded"--no response--nothing happened. Then Elijah built up the altar of the Lord, which was in disrepair. He put the wood upon the altar. Then he put the bullock to be sacrificed upon the wood. Around the altar he had dug a large trench. The he had water poured over the offering and the altar until all was soaked with water and the trench overflowed with water. Then Elijah called upon the God of Abraham and Isaac and Jacob, and the fire of God came down and consumed the altar and the wood and the offering and the water. "And when all the people saw it, they fell on their faces; and they said, The Lord, he is God; the Lord he is God." [I Kings 18:39]

The most significant and impressive demonstration of God's power in human history was in the resurrection of Jesus Christ. Iniquity could take the life of Jesus Christ, but iniquity could not defeat him. Jesus was raised from the dead by the power of God. God demonstrates his power in his mighty works.

How are people properly to respond to the magnificence and grandeur of God? Psalm 1:2 says of the person who trusts in God, "but his delight is in the law of the Lord, and on his law he meditates day and night." As we contemplate the greatness of God, we must recognize that most of us do not direct our thoughts toward God as we should. We allow matters of small import inappropriately to fill out our lives. The result is that much that is best in life is crowded out. It is proper to adore and worship God. There is no one greater than he. Our lives derive from him. Our salvation comes from him. Our destinies are subject to his sovereign will. The knowledge, contemplation, worship, and adoration of God should be at the center of every person's life.

> On the glorious splendor of thy majesty, and on thy wondrous works, I will meditate. Men shall proclaim the might of thy terrible acts, and I will declare thy greatness. They shall pour forth the fame of thy abundant goodness, and shall sing aloud of thy righteousness. [Psalm 145:5-7]

We are to love God with our hearts and souls and minds. We are to seek first the kingdom of God. The other affairs of life are to be subordinate to that grand priority of honoring and adoring God. When people get things in reverse order, they become myopic--the things that are close at hand take on an inappropriate importance. They then fail to see God. They do not sense his glory. They do not praise him and worship him and adore him as it is right and proper to do. When the affairs of life occupy people over much, they become depressed--discouraged--robbed of the glory and joy of life. It is God who gives true joy. Jesus said, "These things I have spoken to you, that my joy may be in you, and that your joy may be full." [John 15:11]

May we love God with all of our hearts! May the majestic triune God be the focus of our attention. Regular Sunday worship is vital to a continuing living relationship with Almighty God. It lays a foundation for the rest of the week. From that weekly beginning we should worship God in our prayers--we should worship God through our study of the Bible--we should worship God with thanksgiving.

The Lord has established his throne in the heavens, and

his kingdom rules over all, Bless the Lord, O you his angels, you mighty ones who do his word, hearkening to the voice of his word! Bless the Lord, all his hosts, his ministers that do his will! Bless the Lord, all his works, in all places of his dominion. Bless the Lord, O my soul!
[Psalm 103:19-22]

"O Lord my God, thou art very great!"

Further Reading

Rhodes, Arnold, *The Mighty Acts of God,* John Knox Press
Psalms 103, 104, 119, 145
Isaiah 55:1-9

For Reflection or Discussion

1. How does the Bible describe God's greatness?

2. What are some of the qualities, abilities, or acts of God that help us to understand his greatness?

3. What are proper responses to the greatness of God?

CHAPTER THREE

THE LOVE OF GOD

In the gospel of John, chapter three, we read about an eminent person coming to speak with Jesus: Nicodemus, a Pharisee, a member of the ruling council of the Jewish nation. Jesus spoke to Nicodemus about his need for true spiritual life--for new birth--for a living relationship with God. That encounter with Nicodemus, and similar instances that we read of in the Bible, might well put a question in our minds. Why should Jesus trouble himself with Nicodemus? Why should Jesus bother with this life at all? How do we explain the statement found in Philippians, chapter two?

> ... who though he was in the form of God, did not count equality with God a thing to be grasped, but emptied himself, taking the form of a servant, being born in the likeness of men. And being found in human form he humbled himself and became obedient unto death, even death on a cross. [Philippians 2:6-8]

Why did God continue engaging in relationships with Adam and Eve, with Noah, with Abraham and Sarah, Isaac, and Jacob, and then with Moses, Joshua, Samuel, David, Asa, Ruth, Esther, and Ezra and, of course many others? What is taking place? What is the meaning of it all?

The answer to these questions is to be found in that text that is at the very heart of the Bible, John 3:16,

> For God so loved the world that he gave his only Son, that whoever believes in him should not perish but have eternal life.

The motive is revealed. It is that God loves the world of people whom he has created. That statement of God's love in John 3:16 is not exceptional. That same motive is frequently affirmed in scripture.

> But God, who is rich in mercy, out of the great love with which he loved us, even when we were dead through our trespasses, made us alive together with Christ...
> [Ephesians 2:4,5]

> In this the love of God was made manifest among us, that God sent his only Son into the world, so that we might live through him. In this is love, not that we loved God but that he loved us and sent his Son to be the expiation for our sins. [I John 4:9,10]

> This is my commandment, that you love one another as I have loved you. Greater love has no man than this, that a man lay down his life for his friends. [John 15:12,13]

> I will recount the steadfast love of the Lord, the praises of the Lord, according to all that the Lord has granted us, and the great goodness to the house of Israel which he has granted them according to his mercy, according to the abundance of his steadfast love. For he said, Surely they are my people, sons who will not deal falsely; and he became their Savior. In all their affliction he was afflicted, and the angel of his presence saved them; in his love and in his pity he redeemed them; he lifted them up and carried them all the days of old. [Isaiah 63:7-9]

The Bible plainly and consistently declares the love of God. That love is marvelous. It is beyond all capacity of understanding and comprehension. God loves every person. God loves people who believe in him. God loves people who do not believe in him. God loves Hispanics, Orientals, Anglos, Africans, Azerbajanians, Bolivinas, Eskimos, and Jews. God loves the world. Jesus came to Earth from heaven because of that inestimable love of God. Because of his intense love, God continues to seek and pursue people, rejoicing when they turn to him. Francis Thompson gave eloquent expression to this in his poem, "The Hound of Heaven":

> I fled Him, down the night and down the days;
> I fled Him, down the arches of the years;
> I fled Him, down the labyrinthine ways
> Of my own mind; and in the midst of tears

The Love of God

I hid from Him, and under running laughter.

Up vistaed hopes I sped; And shot, precipitated
Adown Titanic glooms of chasmed fears,
From those strong Feet that followed, followed after.
But with unhurrying chase,
And unperturbed pace,
Deliberate speed, majestic instancy,
They beat--and a Voice beat
More intent than the Feet--
"All things betray thee, who betrayest Me."

Alack, thou knowest not
How little worthy of any love thou art!
Whom wilt thou find to love ignoble thee
Save Me, save only Me?
All which I took from thee, I did but take,
Not for thy harm
But just that thou might'st seek it in My arms,
All which thy child's mistake
Fancies as lost, I have stored for thee at home;
Rise, clasp My hand, and come"
Halts by me that footfall;
Is my gloom after all,
Shade of His hand, outstretched carresingly?
"Ah, fondest, blindest, weakest,
I am He Who thou seekest!
Thou dravest love from thee, who dravest me."

    God commissioned Jonah to go to Nineveh to warn the people of that city of the imminent judgment of God upon them due to their great wickedness. Jonah was a Jew. He resided in the land of Israel. Nineveh was an alien city. Like many of us, Jonah was a reluctant evangelist. He tried to evade the assignment. But God persisted-- because of his profound and powerful love. He would not let Jonah off the hook until he obeyed. God sent Jonah to Nineveh because he cared about those people. God told Jonah to go to Nineveh to warn them of the consequences of their iniquity. He was to proclaim the severity of the judgment of God; that God would surely destroy Nineveh. When his attempts to elude God failed, having no other choice, Jonah went to Nineveh and preached the message that he had received from God. The people of Nineveh responded to the preaching of Jonah. They repented of their sins, and the king of Nineveh proclaimed that the entire city should exhibit penetance before Almighty God.

Jonah set up camp outside of the city to see when the fire from heaven would come down and consume Nineveh. When the judgment, that Jonah had proclaimed did not come, Jonah was dismayed. He was angry with God. God said to him,

> And should not I pity Nineveh, that great city, in which there are more than a hundred and twenty thousand persons who do not know their right hand from their left, and also much cattle? [Jonah 4:11]

The message of Jonah is simple. Jonah preached to the people of Nineveh, but he did not love them. God loved them.

In the book of Isaiah, as with many of the prophets, we have the word of God rebuking the people that they have broken his covenant with them, and reminding the people of the consequences of their infidelity to God. But alongside of those stern words of warning are the assurances that God is a God of mercy--that God is longsuffering--that God desires the return, the restoration and renewal of those whom he is judging.

> For the mountains may depart and the hills be removed, but my steadfast love shall not depart from you, and my covenant of peace shall not be removed says the Lord who has compassion on you. [Isaiah 54:10]

How was it that Nicodemus came to believe in God? How is it that Peter and James and John and the other apostles believed in God? Why do millions upon millions affirm faith in Jesus Christ today? Is it not that God cares deeply for people? God loves every human being! He initiates the relationship; he makes it possible. He pursues people and enables them to believe in him.

> While we were yet helpless, at the right time Christ died for the ungodly. Why, one will hardly die for a righteous man--though perhaps for a good man one will dare even to die. But God shows his love for us in that while we

The Love of God

> were yet sinners Christ died for us. [Romans 5:6-8]

> ... as Christ loved us and gave himself up for us, a fragrent offering and sacrifice to God. [Ephesians 5:2]

> See what love the Father has given us, that we should be called children of God; and so we are. [I John 3:1]

> Looking to Jesus the pioneer and perfecter of our faith, who for the joy that was set before him endured the cross, despising the shame, and is seated at the right hand of the throne of God. [Hebrews 12:2]

The love of God is unlikely in that, from the divine standpoint, there is nothing in us to love. From the human perspective--to love someone means that there is an inherent worth, attractiveness, and desirability in the person who is loved. But the Bible make it plain that we have none of those qualities.

> None is righteous, no, not one; no one understands, no one seeks for God. All have turned aside, together they have gone wrong; no one does good, not even one. [Romans 3:10-12]

We have not saved ourselves. We cannot save ourselves. God saves people in Jesus Christ--and that out of his love.

As we reflect upon it, we see that God has shown his love for us in many ways. God's love is exhibited in that he has made us in his image. You purchase some seeds and prepare the soil and plant the seeds. You water the prospective plant. Perhaps you provide it with a variety of plant nutrients. You see to it that it gets the proper amount of exposure to the sunlight. You look forward to the emergence of the first shoot and then the development of the plant and finally the plant in full bloom. You have put a lot of interest--we might even say a lot of love--into the development of that plant. Think of the scope of the universe and all that is in it, including the Earth with its abundance of streams, plains, mountains, rivers, oceans, plant, animal, and human life. When God created men and women in his own image, he made them the very crown of his creation! God's work of creation is an act of love.

God loves us in calling those who believe in him his children, his sons and daughters. He loves us in the dignity that he has given to us in Christ. The scriptures affirm that we are joint-heirs of Christ; that Christ is our advocate before the heavenly Father; he is our high priest. He loves us in preparing a place in heaven for us. And he loves us in receiving us unto himself, when it is time for us to depart from this life and enter the heavenly realm.

That love is a special kind of love. We have to be instructed in it by the precept and example of scripture, because it is not something that we understand by nature. We love those with whom we are closely associated. We tend to love those who are responsive to us, and love us in return. But the scriptures teach that God loves us in spite of our unattractiveness in his sight. In our sin, we are unlovely to God. We are not dressed nicely. Our faces are not washed. We do not present ourselves to him with a lovely countenance. Still he loves us!

> But God shows his love for us in that while we were yet sinners Christ died for us   [Romans 5:8]

> For Christ also died for sins once for all, the righteous for the unrighteous, that he might bring us to God,
>   [I Peter 3:18]

Surely, as we believe in Jesus--as we learn of him--as we walk with him--we can learn to love God. But our love follows his love. His love came first. Love begins with God. It is not based on our worth. It is not based on our accomplishments. In large measure, the love of God is a mystery to us. The clearest explanation that the Bible gives to enable our understanding of his love is that he loves us because we are his. He created us for himself. He has a claim upon us. God was the first evangelist. He called Abraham, Isaac, and Jacob and their successors. He sent his Son from heaven to earth to train and commission the twelve so that the whole world would hear the good news of his love. And he enables that witness, which he has commissioned, through the Holy Spirit.

The Love of God

In Luke 15:1,2, we read,

> Now the tax collectors and sinners were all drawing near to hear him. And the Pharisees and the scribes murmured, saying, "This man receives sinners and eats with them."

All four of the gospels tell us that many of the religious leaders of Jesus day were offended at the kinds of people Jesus associated with. In response, Jesus told three parables having to do with the love of God (Luke, chapter 15). It was Jesus' way of saying that if they could understand the love of God, they could understand why he ministered to the sort of people that he did. And if one can understand that principle, then he can understand why Jesus cares for every person.

Jesus told the parable of the man who owned a hundred sheep. Ninety-nine of these sheep were secure in the sheepfold. But one was missing. The shepherd left the ninety-nine and went out looking for the one, because that sheep belonged to him. He wanted to find it. When he found it, he carried it home. He rejoiced more over the one sheep, that he had found, than over the ninety-nine in the fold. God seeks the lost sinner because he loves him.

Jesus told of the woman who had ten coins, and had lost one of them. She might have been consoled. After all, she still had nine left. But she insisted on turning the house upside down looking for the missing coin. When she found it, she invited her friends to celebrate with her. God is delighted when one returns to him, because he loves her.

A man had two sons. One stayed home, and (we presume) did everything that the father required of him. The other son said to the father, in effect, "I'm living a dull life and I am tired of it. I want something exciting. This place is a drag. Let me have my inheritance now, and I will go my own way, and I won't trouble you anymore." The son took his inheritance, and journeyed to a far country whistling all the way. He couldn't leave home soon enough, and he couldn't wait until he arrived at the destination of his dreams. He was going to have a big time! But he lived in dissipation, debauchery, and foolishness. He spent all of his money.

His fair-weather friends were gone. He hired on with a farmer, with the undistinguished job of feeding his pigs, and the food that he had to eat was no better than what the pigs got, and there wasn't enough for him to eat. He was hungry. In his desperation he thought that, perhaps, his father might put him on as a hired hand. He knew that his father's servants were far better off than he was. As he came up the road toward home, the father ran out to greet him. He enfolded him in love. He reinstated him as his son. He threw a big party to celebrate the occasion. The father's love for the son had never been quenched. The love of God is described as graphically in this parable as in any place in the Bible!

When Abraham was at an age when most people are already retired, God called him to pack his bags and move his family. He led Abraham to the land of Caanan. God made a series of incredible promises to Abraham. He promised him that he and his descendants would possess the full extent of the land of Caanan. He promised him that his descendants would be as numerous as the grains of sand by the seashore and the stars in the sky. He further promised that through his offspring the whole world would be blessed. In order to have grandchildren one must have at least one child, and Abraham and Sarah did not have any. They waited and they waited, and finally they tried to fulfill God's promise on their own. Ishmael was the child of Abraham and of Sarah's servant, Hagar. But God did not accept Ishmael, and they continued to wait. Finally, through the miraculous provision of God, Isaac was born to Abraham and Sarah when Abraham was a hundred years old and Sarah was ninety. Through Isaac all of the promises that God had given to Abraham would be fulfilled.

Several years passed after the birth of Isaac. When Isaac was possibly ten or twelve years of age God spoke to Abraham again:

> Take your son, your only son Isaac, whom you love, and go to the land of Moriah, and offer him there as a burnt offering upon one of the mountains of which I shall tell you. [Genesis 22:2]

Abraham was obedient. He took some wood and a knife and his son. They went up to Mount Moriah. There Abraham built an altar. He bound his son and placed him on the altar. He was ready to slay his son in obedience to God, but God stopped him. God does not require human sacrifice of anyone but himself. God was testing Abraham. He wanted to see whom Abraham loved the most. What God did not require of Abraham, he required of himself in the sacrifice of his Son.

> And going a little farther he fell on his face and prayed, My Father, if it be possible, let this cup pass from me; nevertheless, not as I will, but as thou wilt. [Matthew 26:39]

> And about the ninth hour Jesus cried with a loud voice, Eli, Eli, lama sabachthani?" that is, "My God, my God, why hast thou forsaken me?" [Matthew 27:46]

> For our sake he made him to be sin who knew no sin, so that in him we might become the righteousness of God. [II Corinthians 5:21]

> In him we have redemption through his blood, the forgiveness of our trespasses, according to the riches of his grace, which he lavashed upon us. [Ephesians 1:7,8]

> God so loved the world that he gave his only Son.

The third stanza of F. M. Lehman's poem, "The Love of God" is especially powerful:

> Could we with ink the ocean fill
> And were the skies of parchment made
> Were every stalk on earth a quill
> And every man a scribe by trade
> To write the love of God above
>
> Would drain the ocean dry.
> Nor could the scroll contain the whole
> Though stretched from sky to sky.
>
> O love of God, how rich and pure!
> How measureless and strong!
> It shall for evermore endure
> The saints' and angels song.

And then we have the words of Romans, chapter eight:

Who shall separate us from the love of Christ? Shall tribulation, or distress, or persecution, or famine, or nakedness, or peril, or sword? As it is written, "For thy sake we are being killed all the day long; we are regarded as sheep to be slaughtered." No, in all these things we are more than conquerors through him who loved us. For I am sure that neither death, nor life, nor angels, nor height, nor depth, nor anything else in all creation, will be able to separate us from the love of God in Christ Jesus our Lord.
[Romans 8:35-39]

The love of God is unfathomable. It far exceeds our abilities of explanation and description. But the Bible does describe it, and the study of the Bible helps us to realize that it is the greatest of realities. The love of God is manifested in that he created people in his image, in this marvelously designed universe in which he has placed people. But most of all that he has redeemed people through his only begotten Son, Jesus Christ.

Further Reading

Shelly, Bruce L., *Christian Theology in Plain Language,* Word, Chapter 7, "What is God Like?"

Romans 8:12-17

Hebrews 10:5-25

For Reflection or Discussion

1. How is the love of God described or explained?

2. What rationale can one give for the love of God?

3. Can the love of God be explained in relationship to his judgment?

CHAPTER FOUR

THE PROBLEM OF SIN

> If the Lord should suffer the human passions to go to all the lengths to which they are inclined. There is no furious beast, that would be agitated with such ungovernable rage; there is no river, though ever so rapid and violent, that would overflow its boundaries with such impetuosity. In his elect, the Lord heals these maladies by a method which we shall hereafter describe. In others, he restrains them, only to prevent their ebullitions so far as he sees to be necessary for the preservation of the universe. Hence some by shame, and some by fear of the laws, are prevented from running into many kinds of pollutions, though they cannot in any great degree dissemble their impurity; others because they think that a virtuous course of life is advantageous, entertain some languid desires after it, others go further, and display more than common excellence, that by their majesty they may confine the vulgar to their duty. Thus God by his providence restrains the perverseness of our nature from breaking out into external acts, but does not purify it within.
>
> [John Calvin, Institutes]

In addressing the theme of "The Problem of Sin," my goal is not that at the conclusion of this chapter many will henceforth cease from sin; although that would be a worthy goal! To the degree that people are free from sin their lives are better and they are happier. But my point is quite the opposite: that sin is a pervasive problem. It is universal. Every person in the world sins by the exercise of his will. It is a morass from which human beings cannot deliver themselves. Salvation comes from outside the human race; it is a gift of God, and without it people are eternally lost.

> ... for I have already charged that all men, both Jews and Greeks, are under the power of sin, as it is written: None is righteous, no, not one; no one understands, no one seeks for God. All have turned aside, together they have gone wrong; no one does good, not even one." [Romans 3:9-12]

I am using the word, "sin", primarily in its root sense. Not so much in the sense of the sins that we commit (which are admittedly formidable), but of the inner disposition that inexorably produces a multitude of sins. If one had the inclination he could take a basket of oranges and put hooks on them and hang them on an apple tree. But the apple tree would not, thereby, become an orange tree! Nor would the apple tree be sufficiently influenced so that the next season it would produce oranges. Apple trees produce apples because that is their nature. Regretably, we sin because we are sinners. It is of our nature. Only by the grace of God are we delivered from the consequences of our sin!

Sin is endemic. Each person can verify that empirically out of his or her own experience. Any person, who is honest with himself, will have to admit that he does not live up to what he knows to be right. We are not talking about perfecting something that is already quite good--as a master craftsman might put the finishing touches on a piece of fine woodwork. Sin is much more than not measuring up. It is rebellion against God. It is disregard for his law. In its most perverse (and yet common) form, it is turning one's back upon God and choosing to go ones' own way rather than accepting the salvation which he so graciously offers.

Not only is sin confirmed in our own necessary recognition that we do not live as we should, the study of history constantly confronts us with the effects of sin. The reality of sin is also brought home to us in every area of contemporary life as we read the daily newspaper and listen to the news.

> For a hundred years, beginning at Waterloo, the doctrine of the dignity of man was ascendant while the grotesque indignity of death went on claiming a man at a time (and once in a while a large or small batch). We may assume that man's impertinent claim to dignity was an affront to the ancient Enemy. But we may also assume that the Enemy was too old a hand at the game to spend a century of evenings sitting by his ice-cold fire and nursing a pique. If he would bring modern man to heel, he would have to modernize his own procedures and unobtrusively retool. At Verdun he unveiled his own assembly line for mass production.

The Problem of Sin

Two million strapping young men--the apotheosis of Life-- had been driven into a colosseum without spectators and handed the triumphant product of the Age of Man, the machine gun, and set at each other's throats at a distance too great for the distinction of persons or the bestial dignity of the two combatants in the Roman arena. One million of them dutifully killed the other million, and when the million were dead a few hundred yards of mud and blood had changed hands a half-dozen times and the world acknowledged Death as the winner. Mass man had met his mass master and human dignity its indignification. [Milton Mayer, "On Death," *The Great Ideas Today*, 1965, p. 110]

The Bible unequivocally proclaims the fact of sin. Romans 5:12 states,

Therefore, as sin came into the world through one man, and death through sin, and so death spread to all men because all men sinned.

The infection of sin began with our first parents. From them it has spread to the entire race, and only one person has been exempted from that infection: Jesus Christ, our Savior. John wrote, "If we say we have no sin, we deceive ourselves, and the truth is not in us." [I John 1:8] And again, "If we say we have not sinned, we make him a liar, and his word is not in us." [I John 1:10] The reality of sin is not only a fact in the lives of everyone alive today—it is a fact of every human being's life for all of human history from Adam and Eve to the present.

Let us direct our attention to Genesis 3:1-13. This is the initial explanation in the Bible for the presence of sin in the human race. In this present analysis, I am, in part, drawing on the writing of Dr. Addison Leitch in his book, *Interpreting Basic Theology*. Dr. Leitch notes that a series of steps are involved in a person's becoming enmeshed in sin. First, notice that Eve's attention is drawn to the tempter. God ceases to be the center of her attention. Rather her attention has shifted to the devil. The devil speaks to her, and she listens to him. The New Testament warns us to flee temptation. We might add, don't try to convert the devil. You will not be successful. That idea may seem ludicrous now. But, at the outset, it is possible that is what Eve had in mind. If that were so, she overestimated her own capacities. A similar overestimation of our capacities is ordinarily one of our failures when we succumb to sin.

The Bible records for us only two people who directly encountered the devil. The first is Eve; the second is Jesus Christ. And there is a profound difference, if you will examine the two passages. Compare Genesis, chapter 3, with either of the New Testament accounts of the temptation of Jesus (Matthew 4:1-11 or Luke 4:1-13). Eve seeks to reason with the devil. Jesus simply quotes the Old Testament scripture. He does not attempt to engage the devil in argument. We have noted that initially Eve began to pay attention to the devil. The Bible says that if we resist him he will flee from us (James 4:7).

Then the tempter (who is extremely subtle) suggests to her that God is not good. He asked the question, "Did God say, You shall not eat of any tree of the garden?". Do you see what a trap that is? That is not what God said. He said, "You must not eat of the tree of the knowledge of good and evil." Eve foolishly rushes right in: "No sir, you are mistaken. He did not say that." He said rather, "you shall not eat of the fruit of the tree which is in the midst of the garden," (and then she adds) "neither may we touch it lest we die." So far as we have the record in the book of Genesis, God did not say, "do not touch it". He said you will die if you eat of it. That tends to be a very human characteristic when one is playing around with sin. The case is misstated. We make God out to be unreasonable, and we make ourselves, to look as innocent as possible.

The conversation continues. Satan tells an outright lie. He said, "You will not die." The scriptures warn us plainly that the evil one is a liar and the father of lies. Indeed, the New Testament exhorts those who believe in Jesus Christ to have nothing to do with lying, because lying is of the devil. Truth is of God, and those who believe in God should lay hold of the truth and not let go of it. But he lies to her, and she evidently begins to believe his falsehood. In the fifth verse, he makes a very subtle appeal. He says, "God knows that when you eat of it your eyes will be opened, and you will be like God, knowing good and evil."

The Problem of Sin

In our analysis of the subject of temptation, that fifth verse may be the most significant. Because the ultimate temptation is not only to be free from God, but to exercise God's powers. That explains a great deal of the wrongdoing and wickedness of the human race. It is surely Satan's personal ambition, to be like God and to exercise God-like power. It is this god-likeness that he offers to the woman.

We are not told, in the Genesis account, of the length of this conversation. Whether it was a single event or whether it was a series of conversations extending over a substantial period of time. Perhaps initially Eve was very strong, and it took a long time to wear down her will and to change her mind. Perhaps Adam was troubled by these continuing conversations, but was assured by Eve that they did no harm and the she found amusement in them. Whether it was a protracted period of time or a relatively short conversation, we see by the sixth verse that Eve begins to substitute her judgment for the will of God. She eyes that tree. And she affirms to herself that it indeed looks good. It is attractive and appealing, and the fruit appears to be delicious. So she took of the fruit and she ate of it. Dr. Leitch observes,

> All these things are indeed true about the fruit--and all are at this point irrelevant. Many things look good in and of themselves. Still stands the command; we are not to eat. The first question is not ... whether we can see ... that these things are good ...; the question is whether there may be some other things about sin that we can't know just by simple observation and our own ... judgment.

The usefulness of the word of God is that it is true and, therefore, it may be willingly obeyed. More often than not, we are able to discern with our minds the reasons for obeying the word of God. Frequently those reasons are apparent. They are evident. But that is not always the case. The Bible loses its usefulness if one has to figure out why obedience to God requires one to do this or that every time before one acts. If one's reason is sufficient, then the Bible has become superfluous! If we can always figure out on our own what is good for us or what is right and wrong, then we do not need the Bible. All that we need is our reason. Our minds and our rational processes will suffice. But if, indeed, the scriptures are the word of God, then it is especially at those points where we are not clear and lacking in understanding that we need to obey in faith. It is vital to our well being that we learn to obey God.

It is just at this point that Eve departs. She substitutes her mind for the mind of God. She substitutes her will for the will of God. She supposes that she knows better what is good for Eve than God knows. And she decides to act on the basis of her reason. In the process she contracts disaster for herself, for her husband, and for the entire human race. Dr. Leitch goes on to say:

> We are ready and more than ready now for the overt act. Temptation has now led to sin. Temptation and sin are not the same thing, but temptation "played along with" already has sin in it and it is a nice question, many times, as it is in this Genesis account, just where one becomes the other. Potentially, at least, Eve has been on the skids ever since she began believing anything the tempter had to say. Having given her mind and will she now finds no problem in the act.

It is true, temptation, is not sin, but you just keep playing around with temptation and pretty soon you realize that you have crossed the line. You have entered the enemy's territory.

Having sinned herself, Eve now wants to share sin. Is that not a human characteristic? She shares with Adam. He participates with her. Indeed, it is Adam that God ultimately calls to account. They cover themselves with fig leaves and hide from God. Is that not a pitiful and devastating commentary on the human condition? The consequence is (apart from the redemptive work of God in Jesus Christ) people do not feel comfortable in God's presence. They would rather not be confronted by him. They would live without him. A further result is that they often do not feel comfortable with one another. Having become alienated from God their interpersonal relationships also begin to deteriorate.

God comes looking for them and, in a sense, that is the great story of all of the rest of the Bible. God is looking for us! He is seeking us! Every religion other than Christianity is man-made; originated on Earth--not in heaven. The religion of the Bible

The Problem of Sin

rejects the idea of people working their way up to God. The biblical religion is revelation--not the distillation of human wisdom and insight. It is one that has come down from God to us. People have not risen to God. Rather Jesus Christ came from heaven to Earth. God's love is extended toward us. His grace and his mercy are manifest that we might heed his word—accept his offer of forgiveness and believe in Jesus Christ.

God comes looking for them. And what do they do? They hide from him. And then he confronts them. The Lord said to the man, "Where are you?" The man said, "I heard the sound of thee in the garden, and I was afraid because I was naked; and I hid myself." And God said, "Who told you that you were naked? Have you eaten of the tree of which I commanded you not to eat?"
We all ought to hang our heads in shame at the next verse, because it is such a common response! Adam immediately tries to evade his responsibility. He said, "The woman whom thou gavest to be with me, she gave me the fruit of the tree, and I ate." Do you see the implication? First it was the woman and then it was God! "You gave her to me. It is not my fault! It is not my responsibility. It is your responsibility! Ultimately that is what we try to do. We try to shift the responsibility for sin from ourselves to God. We may use sophisticated terms. We may attribute it to heredity or we may blame our environment or we may allege that society is responsible or we may offer up a complex series of causes. But ultimately what we are doing is shifting the responsibility from ourselves to God. "It is the woman, and remember you gave her to me!"

The Lord spoke to the woman, "What is this that you have done?" And she said, "The serpent beguiled me, and I ate." Again, she seeks to avoid responsibility by shifting the blame. God does not buy these evasions. He is the responsible party in this episode. He pronounces judgment on Adam and on Eve. He even pronounces judgment upon the serpent.

I would also note, in concluding commentary on Genesis, chapter 3, that one of the root causes of sin is dissatisfaction. As we read the account of the Garden of Eden we do not read about automobiles and dishwashers and microwaves and stereo sound systems and many other of the "wonders" of twentieth century life. Nonetheless, Adam and Eve had everything that a human being could possibly want. The evil one knew that the way to pry them loose from God was to evoke dissatisfaction. Instead of their thoughts being fixed on what God had given them; instead of contemplating the multitude of blessings that come from God-- they began to focus on what they did not have. From that initial dissatisfaction they began to doubt God's goodness and proceeded to disobey God. From them we have inherited a pernicious tendency toward dissatisfaction and disobedience.

From the human point of view there is no remedy for sin. That irremedialness can be illustrated rather quickly. If you are honest enough to admit that you are a sinner--then just determine to reform. Don't sin anymore! Stop thinking those ugly thoughts. Stop being needlessly critical of others. Stop saying those things that are misleading or harmful or that are better left unsaid. Always act out of love for God and love for your neighbor. We are capable of improvement. But we are incapable of basic reformation. No matter how hard we try, we just cannot make it. Only Jesus could face his enemies and ask, "which of you convicts me of sin." We are incapable of delivering ourselves; incapable of renewing ourselves. And, alas, we cannot forgive ourselves!

If the Bible be removed from consideration, then the entire human race is without hope. The picture is bleak. But the motive for the remedy for sin exists not in you and in me but in God. He loves us. He is compassionate toward us. It is not his will that any should perish but that all should come to believe in him through Jesus Christ. (II Peter 3:9) The remedy for sin is found in the grace of God expressed in the gift of Jesus Christ and his atoning work on the cross. On the cross Jesus bore all of our guilt--all of our iniquity--all of our sin--and all of our judgment. He died for our sins according to the scriptures. The remedy is available, and that is why we can be happy people. We can be joyful because we have the good news that we can come into an eternal living relationship with God.

The world that needs good news can receive it from those who believe in Jesus Christ. Jesus said, I am the way and the truth and the life; no one comes to the Father but by me." [John 14:6] John 5:24 states,

> Truly, truly, I say to you, he who hears my word and believes him who sent me, has eternal life; he does not come into judgment, but has passed from death to life.

Every Sunday in tens of thousands of Christian churches a prayer of confession is offered and a word of pardon is given from the scriptures. We know that God has met our deepest needs in Jesus Christ. In his Son our sins are forgiven. Through Jesus Christ we are given power to live a new life. And in Jesus Christ people have a great future destiny.

> Then he showed me the river of the water of life, bright as crystal, flowing from the throne of God and of the Lamb through the middle of the street of the city; also, on either side of the river, the tree of life with its twelve kinds of fruit, yielding its fruit each month; and the leaves of the tree were for the healing of the nations. [Revelation 22:1,2]

Further Reading

> Calvin, John, *Institutes of the Christian Religion*
> Leitch, Addison H. *Interpreting Basic Theology,* Chapter Five
> Milton, John, *Paradise Lost*
> Isaiah 14:12-20
> Romans 5:12-21
> Romans 7:1-25

For Reflection or Discussion

1. What is sin? What are some basic characteristics of sin?

2. How can the reality of sin be demonstrated?

3. Why does sin present such a serious problem?

4. What is the remedy for sin?

CHAPTER FIVE

THE DEVIL AND THE POWERS OF EVIL

We had a gathering of some of the young adults at the church, and we used our video display unit to view the Walt Disney film "Something Wicked This Way Comes". It was a compelling dramatization of the presence and power of evil. It was also frightening. I would not want young children to see that film. In dealing with the theme of the devil and the powers of evil, it is not my purpose to frighten anyone. Indeed, if after reading this chapter before you retire, you look under the bed or look in the closet to see if the devil or some evil spirit is there, I will have been defeated in my purpose. Because the devil is not a spook. Neither is he the product of childish fantasies. And I doubt that he is in the business of frightening people. Quite the contrary, I think that he likes to work in such a manner that people are unaware of his purposes. He tries to cover his tracks. The Bible says that he is wily and subtle. As II Corinthians 11:14 states, he disguises himself as "an angel of light".

Whittaker Chambers, then a senior editor of Time Magazine wrote a provocative article, "The Devil", that was published in a 1946 issue of Life Magazine. The article and its introduction deal with the clandestine manner in which the devil operates:

> Throughout most of Christian history the Devil was real and personal and never far from the minds of men. But during the last several centuries he has retreated into the realm of myth. Today to most people he is only a joke. Recently, however, several perceptive philosophers have seen him roaming the world and have identified him as the same old Prince of Evil. Among them are Reinhold Niebuhr, C.S. Lewis and Denis de Rougemont, whose comments are quoted on the following pages. On New Year's Eve, a favorite occasion with the Devil, he visited a New York nightclub. There his conversation was overheard by Whittaker Chambers, one of the editors of TIME....

Underground?" said the pessimist.

"My dear fellow," said the Devil, "if what I hear of your background is true, it can be not secret from you that for the last 250 years all Hell has been underground. And I don't mean underground in any narrowly geographic or doctrinal sense. Hell is a conspiracy. Like all good conspiracies, its first requirement is that nobody shall believe in it. Well we have succeeded so well that for centuries there has been no Hell, and there is scarcely a rational man in the world today who, despite the overwhelming evidence to the contrary, believes that the Devil exists."

Several years ago a sixteen year old girl and her mother came into my study in San Jose. This girl, with some other young people, had been involved in the worship of Satan. She was frightened. She wanted to get away from that experience. Although she wanted to be released from any connection with the powers of evil, she was afraid that she could not disengage. She had been in the throes of a very real power, and its potency was such that she was not sure that she could escape. I, of course, urged her to give herself fully to Jesus Christ; to come under his care, and that she would have nothing to fear. Anything having to do with the devil is frightening to some people. But in Jesus Christ it is a matter of being responsible; being realistic. It is a matter of understanding the reality of spiritual powers in their proper perspective. That is, God is the all powerful sovereign who exercises ultimate control.

> Peace I leave with you; my peace I give unto you; not as the world gives do I give to you. Let not your hearts be troubled, neither let them be afraid. [John 14:27]

It is amazing to read some of the Gallup surveys, and to be reminded that substantial numbers of people do not believe in the devil. For example, in Canada, eighty-seven per cent of the people hold a belief in God, but only thirty-seven per cent accept the existence of the devil. In the United States (perhaps for good reason!) there is a higher level of belief in the devil. Sixty-six per cent believe in his existence; twenty-eight per cent say they do not. However, in other countries of the world the situation is quite different. In Great Britain only thirty per cent believe in the existence of the devil; sixty per cent deny his existence. In France seventeen per cent believe that the devil exists; seventy-six per cent do not. A similar situation pertains in the Scandinavian countries. Denmark, Norway, and Sweden register a very low percentage of belief in the reality of the devil.

If someone has a bad dog in their yard, it is imperative that the owners put up a sign to warn of the danger of being attacked and bitten. In such a situation, one has at least been appraised of the danger if he determines to go into the yard with the dog on the loose. Even though people should not have an excessive fear of the devil, they should be alerted to his activities and appreciate the damage that he can do. To continue the analogy: many are being severely attacked and hurt by the devil, but since they are unaware of his existence they erroneously attribute the damage to another source or are mystified by it.

The one who believes in Jesus Christ does not need to fear defeat by Satan. Quite the opposite. He is assured that God does not want him to be defeated. That God has given him adequate resources--and if they are effectively utilized the Christian will stand rather than fall. It is important for people to understand the nature of the contest in which they are engaged. The Bible clearly states that all are confronted with a powerful spiritual adversary. Indeed, unless one recognizes the reality of the spiritual realm: of God and his purposes and of the ultimate triumph of the kingdom of God and the temporary presence of the powers of evil--much of what occurs (that might be understood) will be inscrutable.

Life has a spiritual dimension, and it is out of that spiritual dimension (God's realm) that life flows. God willed; God spoke and the material universe came into being. The best people in the Bible have always understood that God's realm is the most important. The writer to the Hebrews said of Abraham, "For he looked forward to the city which has foundations, whose builder and maker is God." [Hebrews 11:10] Abraham looked forward to that time when he would be with God, and this profoundly influenced the way that he lived. The prospect of entering into God's realm had an impact on every area of his life. Moses, David, Isaiah, Jeremiah, and the apostles cannot be understood unless one recognizes that they gave primary regard to God's kingdom. The reality of the spiritual realm impinges upon this life, and one's recognition or lack of recognition of that reality profoundly affects the way that one lives.

Both history and contemporary events provide abundant evidence of the reality of the powers of evil. Before World War I hundreds of thousands of Armenians were massacred by the Turks. The systematic extinguishing of the lives of five to six million Jews and also of tens of thousands of Gypsies and Slavs by Nazi Germany will surely never be erased from human memory. The ones who committed those egregious atrocities were not uncivilized barbarians. Many of them were people who loved great music and who collected magnificent paintings. A notable number were patrons of the arts and sciences. Their forebears had produced some of the world's great literature and music. Some of the most advanced science has been nurtured within that German culture. Yet out of that framework came some of the most terrible atrocities that have ever been committed in human history.

The "Holocost" points not just to a German problem, but to a human problem. We do not know how many people were systematically exterminated in Cambodia after the ending of the Viet Nam conflict. The estimates range from one to three million in a country with a total population that did not exceed seven million. In 1985 the Los Angeles area wa terrorized by Richard Rimirez, "the Night Stalker". It is not known precisely how many murders he committed, but they appear to have exceeded fifteen in number. Rimirez is an avowed worshiper of Satan. A year does not go by without the report of several such grisley homicidal rampages.

Many commentators have said that the smuggling of drugs into the United States and the use of drugs by the population of the United States is a national emergency on the scale of a major war. In 1986 the United States sent some of its military personnel to Bolivia in a desperate attempt to reduce the problem of the drug traffic originating from that country. More than a half million persons are said to have been killed in the useless war between Iran and Iraq with total casualties numbering well over one million. There were more dead and wounded in the Iran/Iraq War than in the tragic American Civil war.

Child battering is on a scale that can scarcely be contemplated. There are more than 120,000 cases of child abuse in the State of California each year. Approximately one and a half million abortions are performed annually in the United States. Surely the practice of abortion, on this scale, is a great evil. The Los Angeles Times reported that one out of every thirty-five males in the United States are either in prison, in jail, or on probation or parole. Newsweek magazine reported that experts estimate employees steal from $40 to 100 billion per year in the United States. The Savings and Loan Crisis that became so notorious in the United States in 1988 and 1989 is primarily attributable to misappropriation, fraud, and embezzlement.

The existence of evil should be apparent. It is not just an unexplainable aberration. It has a cause. The ultimate source of evil is Satan and his minions. People should be aware that there is an enemy of their souls. We read in I Peter 5:8, "Be sober, be watchful, your adversary, the devil, prowls around like a roaring lion seeking someone to devour." Eve, the mother of us all, knew the devil to be real. Jesus, although himself without sin, nonetheless, encountered the evil one. Simon Peter experienced his malign influence. We read in Luke 22:31,32, when Jesus said,

> Simon, Simon, behold, Satan demanded to have you, that he might sift you like wheat, but I have prayed for you that your faith may not fail;

We read in Revelation 12:17,

> Then the dragon was angry with the woman, and went off to make war on the rest of her offspring, on those who keep the commandments of God and bear testimony to Jesus.

There is a very real sense in which if one believes in Jesus Christ and seeks to follow him--the conflict with evil will be more acute. The scriptures warn that every believer is engaged in a spiritual conflict, but they also give guidance and encouragement. The Bible says, be strong in the Lord and in the strength of his might. Put on the whole armor of God, that you may be able to stand against the wiles of the devil. [Ephesians 6:10,11]

It is not God's purpose that those who trust in him succumb to the powers of evil. Nor is it his purpose that they be inappropriately intimidated by those powers. Rather by trusting in God through obedience to his word, and by laying hold of the spiritual equipment that he makes readily available, the Christian will be strengthened for those tests which will continue throughout each lifetime. The scriptures inform us as to the strategies of the devil. We should be on guard against them:

1. *He misrepresents God.* Remember what he said to Eve in the garden, "Did God say, You shall not eat of any tree of the garden?" Satan misrepresented the case. He will lie and distort the truth to his advantage.

2. *He is a liar and a deceiver.* He is called "The deceiver of the whole world." Revelation 12:9,

> And the great dragon was thrown down, that ancient serpent, who is called the Devil and Satan, the deceiver of the whole world—he was thrown down to the earth, and his angels were thrown down with him.

The apostle Paul, following his call by Jesus Christ, went out into the Greek and Roman world proclaiming the good news of Christ. God mightily used him, churches were founded, and thousands believed in Jesus. Inevitably, there were false teachers who hounded him undermining and eroding the work that he did. Paul wrote about this to the church at Corinth,

> For such men are false apostles, deceitful workmen, disguising themselves as apostles of Christ. And no wonder, for even Satan disguises himself as an angel of light. So it is not strange if his servants also disguise themselves as servants of righteousness. Their end will correspond to their deeds. [II Corinthians 11:13-15]

People are misled when they follow false teaching, and thus the falsehoods of the evil one, rather than the truth of God. The devil is a liar and a deceiver. Jesus said of him,

> He was a murderer from the beginning, and has nothing to do with the truth, because there is no truth in him. When he lies, he speaks according to his own nature, for he is a liar and the father of lies. [John 8:44]

Whether one recognizes it or not, all have been deceived by him. All of us, at one time or another, like Eve have believed his lies rather than God's truth.

3. *He seeks to keep people from the word of God:* Jesus told the parable of the sower and the seed. The sower sowed the seed, and as was characteristic in the areas of planting in his day, some of it fell upon the path and was trampled under foot. Some of it fell upon soil that was too shallow. The seed rapidly germinated and the plants sprang forth, but there was not enough soil to sustain its growth. Other of the seed fell upon good soil and grew, but there was a profusion of weeds and other extraneous plants to choke it out. Still other seed fell on good soil, and produced an abundant crop. The disciples did not understand that parable. And Jesus explained, "Satan immediately comes and takes away the word which is sown in them." The seed is the word of God. Satan seeks to deprive people of the word of God.

What are the causative factors behind the statistics, previously cited, of the non-belief of many people in the devil? Probably the basic cause of this ignorant and misinformed condition is that many do not read the Bible. They do not know what it says. The problem is exacerbated in that many people have decided opinions about the Bible even when they have not read it. Many, who have little or no knowledge of the Bible, presume themselves to be adequately informed as to its contents. A sound knowledge of the scriptures is a primary line of defense, provided by God, against the powers of evil. The believer should read the Bible devotedly every day. The scriptures should be at the very center of one's life. We have noted that the devil seeks to keep people from the word of God. We might ask, has the devil been successful in keeping you from God's word? That is his aim. It is to separate you from the word of God--and, thus, ultimately to separate you from God.

4. *He seeks to lead people into active disobedience of God.* That is what he was doing with Adam and Eve. That is what he succeeded in with Simon Peter, as Peter three times denied his Savior. We read that when Judas betrayed Jesus, Satan entered his heart. When Paul talked about the undermining of the work of God, as the gospel was proclaimed, he saw Satan as the source of that undermining. The devil seeks to alienate people from God by getting them to disobey God. His methodologies remain the same. There is no reason for him to change, because the same formulas continue to work for him: the appeal of power, money, passion, and pride. He methodically works those same themes over year after year, generation after generation, person after person, and they continue to be productive.

5. *He seeks to disrupt Christian unity.* He sends false teachers seeking to lead those within the Christian community astray, seeking to divide them, seeking to undermine legitimate Christian leadership.

6. *He physically afflicts those who believe in God.* In Luke, chapter 13, we read of a woman, "Who had spirit of infirmity for eighteen years; she was bent over and could not fully straighten herself." Jesus referred to her as "a daughter of Abraham whom Satan bound for eighteen years,". Recall the story of Job. Humanly speaking, Job was one of the finest persons who have ever lived. God said to Satan (Job, chapter one),

> Have you considered my servant Job, that there is none like him on the earth, a blameless and upright man, who fears God and turns away from evil?

And Satan said (I am using my own words), "Give me a crack at him." And he afflicted Job severely. In II Corinthians, chapter 12, Paul talks about his thorn in the flesh. He referred to it as a "messenger of Satan". The evil one afflicted him, but God used that affliction to his glory. It only caused Paul to trust more completely and fully in Christ. The Bible confidently assures us that we have adequate resources in this conflict. What a marvelous assurance is I Corinthians 10:13,

> No temptation has overtaken you that is not common to man. God is faithful, and he will not let you be tempted beyond your strength but with the temptation will also provide the way to escape, that you may be able to endure it.

Most of us are guilty of great rationalizations in the arena of personal temptation. When we are tempted--when we want to do something that we would like to do that we really know we should not do--we rationalize that we are a special case and that we are under greater pressure than anyone has ever been in the whole history of the world! That ours is a unique situation. The Bible says that is not so! The temptations that you experience are the same sort that millions of other people experience. If you are trusting in God, he will not allow you to be tempted beyond your endurance. James wrote, "Submit yourselves therefore to God. Resist the devil and he will flee from you." [James 4:7] We read in Ephesians 4:27, "give no opportunity to the devil."

Finally, marvelous God-given resources are listed for us in Ephesians, chapter six. God has given six items of spiritual equipment to enable those who trust in him to stand against the powers of evil:

1. *The truth* (6:14): The Christian should value the truth. He should not tamper with it. He should not compromise it away. He should not rationalize that sometimes it is useful to tell a lie.. When we use the techniques of the adversary, we play into his hands aligning ourselves with him rather than with God. Jesus said, "you will know the truth, and the truth will make you free." Jesus always spoke the truth. He did not mislead. He was always honest. A firm commitment to the truth of God facilitates the strengthening of God.

2. *The equipment of the gospel* (6:15): The gospel brings the knowledge that one is loved of God, that people are forgiven in Jesus Christ, that salvation is a gift--it is not something that is merited or earned; that one has eternal life in Jesus Christ. Your reception of the gospel helps you to maintain your allegiance to God, not to

disobey him, and not to be wayward.

3. *Faith* (6:16): On the one hand faith is a gift of God. But it is also like a muscle. It is vitally important that one exercise his faith, and thus increase in his trust of God. "So faith comes from what is heard, and what is heard comes by the preaching of Christ." [Romans 10:17]

4. *Salvation* (6:17): In most athletic contests, the best defense is a good offense. If your team has the ball or the puck and is attacking the opponent's goal--then they will not be attacking your goal. The person who is actively sharing Jesus Christ, seeking to serve God, seeking to fulfill his will, will be much less susceptible to the wiles of the devil.

5. *The word of God* (6:17): I have already mentioned the importance of regular Bible study in the believer's life. Satan fears it. The believer should love it. Every Christian should make the regular study of scripture a vital part of his life. It is "the sword of the Spirit". One gains skill with a sword through practice and use. It is the individual study of the Bible, and then studying the Bible with others, and then talking to all kinds of people about the Bible--that helps to increase one's skill so that it can be used with increasing effect.

6. *Prayer* (6:18,19):

> Pray at all times in the Spirit, with all prayer and supplication. To that end keep alert with all perseverance making supplication for all the saints, and also for me, that utterance may be given me in opening my mouth boldly to proclaim the mystery of the gospel.

We are to glorify God in prayer. We are to give thanks to God in prayer. We are to pray for deliverance from temptation. We are to pray for our brothers and sisters in Christ. We are to pray for the extension of the gospel to the end that workers go into the harvest fields and many hearts are turned to Christ. As we pray, God delivers us from evil. It is his plan that the believer stand, that he not succumb to the allurements of evil.

> For whatever is born of God overcomes the world; and this is the victory that overcomes the world, our faith. Who is it that overcomes the world but he who believes that Jesus is the Son of God? [I John 5:4,5]

God does not intend the defeat of his children. He looks for their victory. And he said to them, "I saw Satan fall like lightning from heaven." [Luke 10:18] The armor of God is the loving provision of God for our well being. Every believer must fully avail himself of it!

Further Reading

Adler, Mortimer J. *The Angels and Us*, Collier Books (Macmillan)
Emerging Trends, Princeton Religion Research
Lewis, C.S., *Screwtape Letters*
Job 1:1-2:8

For reflection or discussion

1. If God is supreme, why did he allow Satan to harm Job?

2. What are some current manifestations of evil that point to the presence of the devil?

3. Is the devil more of a problem for Christians than for non-Christians?

4. What keeps Christians from making better use of "the whole armor of God"?

5. What are some of the more effective tactics used by the devil in the present day?

CHAPTER SIX

DIVINE JUDGMENT

It was a hot summer afternoon in the land of Caanan, and Abraham, having fulfilled many of his tasks for the day, sat outside of his tent. In the distance he could see three men making their way toward him, and as they came closer he must have eyed them with considerable curiosity. When they approached, he arose, introduced himself, and bade them be his guests. He surely recognized that these were no ordinary strangers. He had a meal prepared for them, and they ate with him. Afterward they told him the good news that Sarah, who had never born a child, was to have a son, in spite of the fact that she was now ninety years old. In due course, Sarah conceived and Isaac was born.

The three visitors had other information for Abraham as well. They told him that their continuing mission was to bring the judgment of God upon two of the cities of the Jordan valley, Sodom and Gomorrah. At that point in the conversation there is a wonderful interchange between Abraham and the angel of God. Affirming that God must always do right, Abraham inquired if God would not be restrained if he found fifty righteous persons in Sodom. The Lord assured him that in such a case he would not destroy the city. Pleading for God to be patient with him, Abraham asked what the case would be if forty-five righteous were found; then he asked regarding forty; then of thirty; then of twenty; and finally of ten. In each instance the Lord assured Abraham that he would not destroy the city for the sake of the righteous persons therein. Then the visitors went their way. Sodom and Gomorrah and related cities were destroyed as a consequence of God's judgment upon their notorious iniquity. Some observers might have concluded that it was a volcanic eruption or that the destruction was the result of an earthquake or other natural phenomena. But we are told, on the authority of scripture, that the devastation of these cities was the result of divine judgment (whatever the apparent or "natural" cause may have been).

More than five hundred years after that event, Abraham's descendants, now numbering in the hundreds of thousands were in Egypt. Although their ancestors originally had been welcomed into Egypt, the situation had profoundly changed. Fearful of their growing numbers, the Egyptians had made slaves of the people of Israel. God had appointed Moses, with his brother Aaron, as his spokesman to confront Pharaoh to the end that the people of Israel might be released from their slavery. They told Pharaoh that it was the will of the One God that the people of Israel be allowed to leave Egypt that they might properly worship him. On several occasions Pharaoh appeared to accede to their requests-- only to relent and later refuse to keep his promises. In resisting Moses and Aaron, Pharaoh was resisting God. The result of Pharaoh's obstinacy was a series of nine dreadful plagues, that fell upon the Egyptians in increasing severity until in the terrible final act of judgment the angel of the Lord slew the first born in every household in Egypt.

About a year after the exodus from Egypt the people of Israel were in the Sinai wilderness. Moses was on Mount Sinai for a period of forty days and forty nights. There he received from God the Ten Commandments, the laws and ordinances of God for Israel the plan for the construction of the Tabernacle, and the system whereby Israel was to worship God. During that forty day period the people of Israel grew restless:

> When the people saw that Moses delayed to come down from the mountain, the people gathered themselves together to Aaron, and said to him, "Up, make us gods, who shall go before us; as for this Moses, the man who brought us up out of the land of Egypt, we do not know what has become of him." [Exodus 2:1]

Aaron caved in to the idolatrous inclinations of his people. They brought gold jewelry, and from it Aaron cast a golden calf. The people bowed down to worship the calf, and having been temporarily freed from the true God, "the people sat down to eat and drink, and rose up to play." When Moses came down from the mountain and saw their faithlessness, he was so angered that he threw down the tablets of the law, given to him by God, and broke them. He rebuked the people--he burned the calf with fire-- ground it to powder--scattered it upon the water--and made the people drink the water. Three thousand men were slain by the swords of the sons of Levi, and God sent a plague upon the people in further judgment for their sins.

Divine Judgment

The people of Israel congealed into a nation in the Sinai wilderness and there God established his covenant with them. As they were faithful to God, as they kept his covenant, God blessed them and prospered them and made a great nation of them. But when they turned to the idols of the peoples around them, when they disregarded the law of God, when they ignored the covenant that God had made with them--the severity of God's judgment fell upon them. Their land became scorched and unproductive through lack of rain. Locusts and other insects devoured their crops. They died from plagues, and they suffered defeat after defeat before their enemies. Finally they were exiled from their homeland and scattered throughout the world. The Assyrians, the Babylonians, the Persians, and finally the Greeks under Alexander the Great and his successors, became instruments of God's judgment upon the people of Israel.

We move on from the Old Testament to the time of Jesus and read a significant incident in Luke, chapter 13. People have not changed much from that time to this. They are fascinated by the tragedies that befall others. The disciples asked Jesus about an item that was in the news of that day:

> There were some present at that very time who told him of the Galileans whose blood Pilate had mingled with their sacrifices.

Undoubtedly something had offended the Romans and, in order to teach the Jews a lesson, Pilate had ordered the slaughter of innocent people by his soldiers. Jesus used that incident to warn his hearers that all must be ready to respond to a holy God:

> Do you think that these Galileans were worse sinners than all the other Galileans, because they suffered thus I tell you, No; but unless you repent you will all likewise perish.
> [Luke 13:2,3]

Apparently the inclination of that time, and of this day as well, is to attribute some hidden wrong to people who are the victims of such tragedies. In the minds of those who inquired of Jesus, perhaps those slaughtered by Pilate were especially deserving of the judgment of God! We might have preferred if Jesus had assured them that this atrocity by Pilate was in no sense God's judgment. But, as the record stands, Jesus did not do that. Rather he uses the occasion to affirm the certainty of the judgment of God, and, therefore, that all should repent of their sins and seek God's forgiveness and mercy. That is, both those who asked the question and those who were the victims of Pilate's ruthlessness.

The theme of judgment is a major emphasis of scripture. However, it is not a fashionable or popular one at present. In fact, it is so out of fashion that many otherwise orthodox Christian ministers ignore it altogether! But the doctrine of salvation--the cross of Christ--the suffering of Christ--all become unintelligible without the background of the judgment of God. Without an understanding of the certainty of God's judgment, the drama of the communion service (the Eucharist) is lost. The love of God is reduced to sheer sentimentalism if his determination to judge is not comprehended.

God's holiness, his righteousness, his justice and, therefore, his utter intolerance of evil is affirmed from the beginning to the end of the Bible.

> But by that same word the heavens and earth that now exist have been stored up for fire, being kept until the day of judgment and destruction of ungodly men.
> [II Peter 3:7]

In the Gospel of John, chapter five, Jesus not only clearly affirms the fact of judgment--but he states that he will himself exercise that judgment.

> For as the Father has life in himself, so he has granted the Son also to have life in himself, and has given him authority to execute judgment, because he is the Son of man.
> [John 5:26,27]

Judgment was the frequent theme of the apostle Paul as he spoke to the Jews and godfearers in synagogues throughout the Greek/Roman world, and as he addressed Gentiles in public places. When in Athens, during his second missionary journey, he gave a stern warning to his hearers,

> The times of ignorance God overlooked, but now he commands all men everywhere to repent, because he has fixed a day on which he will judge the world in righteousness by a man whom he has appointed, [Acts 17:30,31]

While in Roman custody in Caesarea, Paul stood before the Roman governor, Felix, who was apparently fascinated by much that Paul had to say, but troubled when Paul spoke to him of the judgment of God.

> And as he argued about justice and self-control and future judgment, Felix was alarmed and said, "Go away for the present; when I have an opportunity I will summon you." [Acts 24:24,25]

The book of Hebrews warns that even the "religious" person must not presume upon God's goodness:

> For if we sin deliberately after receiving the knowledge of the truth, there no longer remains a sacrifice for sins, but a fearful prospect of judgment, and a fury of fire which will consume the adversaries. A man who has violated the law of Moses dies without mercy at the testimony of two or three witnesses. How much worse punishment do you think will be deserved by the man who has spurned the Son of God, and profaned the blood of the covenant by which he was sanctified, and outraged the spirit of grace? [Hebrews 10:26-29]

Charles Hodge, a theologian from an earlier generation at Princeton Theological Seminary, wrote,

> The Scriptures abound in passages which set forth God as the moral ruler of men; which declare that He will judge the world in righteousness. The Bible represents Him as the judge of nations and individuals; as the avenger of the poor and the persecuted. It abounds also in promises and in threatenings and in illustrations of the righteous judgments of God. Nothing, therefore, is plainer than that men in this world are subject to the moral government of God. Besides this, the Bible also teaches that there is a future

state of reward and punishment; in which the inequalities and anomalies here permitted shall be adjusted.

The *International Standard Bible Encyclopaedia* states in part,

> In Christian theology the Last Judgment is an act in which God interposes directly into human history, brings the course of this world to a final close, determines the eternal fate of human beings, and places them in surroundings spiritually adapted to their final condition.
> [*ISBE,* vol. III, p. 1777]

The historic creeds and confessions of the church consistently state their understanding that the scriptures teach that God distinguishes between those who believe in him and those who do not; that he rewards those who are faithful to him--and eternally separates from himself those who reject him.

> And he shall come again with glory to judge both the quick and the dead,... [The Nicene Creed]

> ... from thence he shall come to judge the quick and the dead. [The Apostles' Creed]

> We believe that the same Lord Jesus shall visibly return for this Last Judgment as he was seen to ascend. And then, we firmly believe, the time of refreshing and restitution of all things shall come, so that those who from the beginning have suffered violence, injury, and wrong, for righteousness' sake, shall inherit that blessed immortality promised them from the beginning. But, on the other hand, the stubborn, disobedient, cruel persecutors, filthy persons, idolators, and all sorts of the unbelieving, shall be cast into the dungeon of utter darkness, where their worm shall not die, nor their fire be quenched. [*The Scots Confession,* Chapter XI]

> The kingdom of heaven is opened when it is proclaimed and openly testified to believers, one and all, according to the command of Christ, that as often as they accept the promise of the gospel with true faith all their sins are truly forgiven them by God for the sake of Christ's gracious

work. On the contrary, the wrath of God and eternal condemnation fall upon all unbelievers and hypocrites as long as they do not repent. It is according to this witness of the gospel that God will judge the one and the other in this life and in the life to come. [The Heidelberg Catechism, Part II]

Some would have us believe that the concept of judgment may be appropriate for the Old Testament, but that it is not congenial to the New Testament. However, many of the passages on the theme of judgment, previously referred to in this chapter, are from the New Testament. To separate the theme of judgment from the teachings of Jesus would render his teachings virtually unintelligible. Jesus emphasized over and over again the importance of choosing for God and not following the course of this world. In many of his parables, Jesus taught the urgency of responding to God while it is opportune. Severe consequences befall those who fail to respond.

1. The parable of the five wise and the five foolish young women (Matthew 25:1-13). The five wise young women took flasks of oil with their lamps. When the bridegroom arrived they were ready, and they went in with him to the marriage feast. The five foolish young women delayed providing oil for their lamps. They were unprepared for the arrival of the bridegroom, and consequently were excluded from the marriage feast. When taken with similar parables and the rest of the teachings of Jesus, the intent of Jesus here is quite plain that to delay responding to God is to say, in effect, to God that we have more important matters to tend to. Such a spirit is the heart of unbelief and disregard for God. It will be rewarded by exclusion from the master's presence.

2. The parable of the five, two, and one talents (Matthew 25:14-30). This parable has to do with three servants to whom their master entrusted a portion of his property. To one he gave five talents, to another two, and to another one. The one, who had received the five talents, traded and made five talents more. Similarly the one who had received the two talents gained two talents more. But the one who had received the one talent did nothing with it. After a long time their master returned. He commended the first two servants who had made good use of their opportunity. But the servant who had squandered his spiritual opportunity was judged severely. Jesus makes it clear that to do

nothing in regard to God is to court spiritual disaster.

> And cast the worthless servant into the outer darkness; there men will weep and gnash their teeth
> [Matthew 25:30]

3. The parable of the great banquet (Luke 14:16-24). A person of importance gave a great banquet and invited many. There is more than a touch of irony in this parable, because it portrays the sort of social event that people love to attend, long to be invited to, and are envious when others are invited and they are not. The series of excuses and rejections that follow are incredible. No person in his or her right mind would reject such an opportunity. The outcome is that those who have rejected the invitation are excluded, and others are invited. It is apparent that God judges. He distinguishes between those who respond and those who do not respond to his gracious invitation.

4. The parable of the wheat and the tares (Matthew 13:24-30). A man sowed good seed in his field, but while his workmen slept an enemy came and sowed weeds among the wheat. The weeds and the wheat were allowed to grow together until the harvest. At the harvest the weeds were separated from the wheat. The wheat was gathered into the master's barn and the weeds were burned. When taken in context with the other teachings of Jesus, this is quite evidently a parable of judgment. I realize there are those who take parables like this and derive secondary meanings from them, which may be helpful. Still others draw imaginative, fanciful, and far fetched interpretations from these parables that may exhibit the cleverness or the originality of the person offering such an interpretation, but they obfuscate the basic and plain meaning of the parable. The basic meaning here is quite plain: God distinguishes between those who are true to him and those who are not, and the consequences are ultimate.

5. The parable of the net that was cast into the sea (Matthew 13:47-50). Fishermen cast their net into the sea and draw it in again. They keep the good fish and throw away those that are not useful to them. Jesus is quite explicit as to the meaning of this parable, and he, thereby, makes the point of similar parables quite clear:

So it will be at the close of the age. The angels will come out and separate the evil from the righteous, and throw them into the furnace of fire; there men will weep and gnash their teeth. [Matthew 13:50]

6. Jesus, teaching of the judgment between the sheep and the goats (Matthew 25:31-46). This is not a parable, but it is closely associated with the two parables previously cited from Matthew, chapter 25. In this passage Jesus teaches an absolute distinction between those who do acts of kindness in his name and those who do not. The point of this teaching is not the means of salvation, but the evidence--the fruits of salvation. Those who are faithful to Christ will do acts of kindness; those who are unfaithful will not. The separation is absolute, and the judgment is eternal.

The concept of judgment, the separation of the righteous from the unrighteous is basic and elementary throughout the Bible. The injustices of this life, which are many, demand resolution. If they are not to be resolved--then life is deprived of meaning. Any true moral or ethical values are lost as well. The Bible promises that God will settle the accounts, "Vengeance is mine, I will repay, says the Lord." [Romans 12:19]

The theme of judgment is not a popular one. Because all people are sinners, every person is vulnerable before the judgment seat of God. Because of that, there are innumerable attempts to wish away or rationalize God's judgment. There is a perverse spirit within people that would like to live without interference from God. But to follow that inclination is to pursue disaster. People cannot live their lives well without God. The more carefully we study the lives of individuals, societies and nations, and the entirety of human history--the more apparent should it be that people cannot make it on their own without God. Human presumption, arrogance, and hubris are abundant, but inappropriate. The record does not sustain human pride and unbridled optimism. The theme of judgment should be approached soberly and rationally recognizing that the authority for judgment is in God's hands--not ours.

If God did not judge, it would be plain that he does not care how people live, what they do, or how they treat one another. The Bible makes it quite clear that God cares very much about these matters. If God did not judge--evil would be on an equal footing with righteousness! An even worse possibility is that people would lose their ability to distinguish between good and evil. If there is no righteousness and justice--then there is no goodness--and if there is not goodness then how is heaven possible? If there is not judgment then, perhaps, the "worst" people who have ever lived are right and the "best" people who have ever lived are wrong.

One of the main purposes of the knowledge of the judgment of God is to encourage godly and righteous living. The fact of the judgment of God is to make it plain to all people that they are morally corrupt, that they cannot save themselves, that they need a Savior. Awareness of the judgment of God should lead people to repent of their sins and plead God's mercy and forgiveness, which he graciously offers in Jesus Christ.

The rebuttal to the apparent harshness of the judgment of God is the grace and mercy that God extends to all through his Son. Like the five wise young women--we should not procrastinate, postpone, or delay. If God cares for us, should we not care about him? If, indeed, Christ died for us on the cross, can we rightly treat it as of little account? One ignores God at his peril! It is right and proper for people to put oil in their lamps, to believe in Jesus Christ, to commit themselves to the God who loves them and graciously invites their commitment. That commitment is not optional. It is essential.

Some arguments made against the judgment of God

1. It is too severe. The punishment is out of proportion to the crime. Divine judgment for a limited time period would be more appropriate.

Answer: Who is to determine the appropriateness of judgment other than God? Who is more fit than God to render ultimate judgment? Similar criticisms or questions may underestimate the reality and persistence of evil; the recalcitrance of many to persist in their own way rather than in God's way.

2. God is love. His character will guarantee that he will forgive everyone of their sins. Because of the wonderful love of God, no one will be excluded from heaven.

Answer: The same Bible that declares the love of God also declares his holiness, righteousness, and justice. It is inconsistent to affirm the one theme and to deny the other. It is impossible for a finite human being to say that love and judgment are irreconcilable in an infinite God. It is erroneous to draw logical inferences from the proposition of the love of God that are plainly contrary to what the Bible teaches.

3. Ignorance: some have never had the opportunity to hear of salvation in Jesus Christ and to respond.

Answer: The Bible teaches that all people willingly do what they know to be wrong, and are guilty before God. The Bible does teach a difference in judgment between those who willfully, knowingly disobey God and those who act out of ignorance. While the Bible gives no argumentation regarding the fate of those who have genuinely not had the opportunity to hear--it does assure us that God is impartial and absolutely just.

Further Reading

Bloesch, Donald G., *Essentials of Evangelical Theology*, Vol 2, Chap IX, "Heaven and Hell", Harper & Row
Hebrews 3:7-9, 6:1-8, 10:26-29
Lincoln, Abraham, "Second Inaugural Address"
Lewis, C. S., *The Problem of Pain*

For Reflection or Discussion

1. If God did not judge, what would the alternatives be?

2. What is the best response to those who accuse God of unrighteousness in judgment?

3. Give three reasons against the concept of divine judgment.

4. Give three reasons supporting the concept of divine judgment.

CHAPTER SEVEN

SALVATION IN JESUS CHRIST

Salvation is a comprehensive term involving many facets. It is important to be precise in one's definition. It involves at least all of the following concepts: faith/belief/commitment, repentance, forgiveness of sins, new birth (regeneration), adoption, sanctification, and glorification. It is not uncommon for Christians to speak as if their salvation was a past event. What they mean is that their initial faith/commitment occurred at some past point in time. But the whole of salvation is an ongoing process (with a beginning on which a person may legitimately place a high value) that continues with the believer joined with Christ in celestial glory.

In this chapter I ordinarily use the term, "salvation", in a general or popular sense to signify the reception of the forgiven sinner through faith into an eternal living relationship with Almighty God. In this sense, salvation is the restoration of a broken relationship between God and those who come to trust in him through Jesus Christ. From one perspective the Christian religion is not at all simple. The many grand themes contained in the sixty-six books of the Bible are formidable. The themes of law and grace, the sovereignty of God and the free will and moral accountability of people, the love of God and the judgment of God, the program of God for this age and the next, the transcendence and immanence of God, the marvelous attributes of God-- are all so vast that one surely could spend a lifetime of study in each of them.

Closer to the subject of this chapter are the processes by which a person learns to believe in Jesus Christ and learn to be faithful to him. There is an enigma here. If there is complexity to the whole of the biblical message, there is also great simplicity. That simplicity is well expressed in John 3:16: "For God so loved the world that he gave his only Son, that whoever believes in him should not perish but have eternal life."

While the apostle Paul was on the second missionary journey he received a vision from God leading him to go from Asia Minor to Macedonia. Some time after Paul and Silas had arrived in

Philippi, the capital of Macedonia, they were unjustly accused, humiliated, beaten, and jailed. At midnight they were singing hymns and praising God. Then there was a great earthquake, and the pagan jailer thought that he had lost his prisoners. He knew that such a loss was considered inexcusable, and that his punishment would be severe. So he determined to take his own life. But Paul called out from the darkness urging him not to harm himself. Paul assured him that all of the prisoners remained in the jail. The jailer suddenly and dramatically realized that life after all has meaning, and that he must be in a right relationship with the God who had created him. He entered the jail and fell trembling with fear before Paul and Silas. He said, "Men, what must I do to be saved." They did not engage in a lengthy theological discourse. They did not give him a book to read. They did not give instruction in how one may become a good Presbyterian, Baptist, or Lutheran! They said, "Believe in the Lord Jesus, and you will be saved, you and your household." [Acts 16:32]

The simplicity of the Christian religion is striking: Trust in Jesus Christ--accept him as your Savior--and you are forgiven of your sins and adopted into God's family. John 3:16, John 5:24, Romans 3:23,24, Romans 10:9,10, Ephesians 2:8,9, and many other passages are small doors--yet they provide an entry point into a wide and marvelous world; God's world.

In dealing with the subject of salvation, the scriptures either assume or directly state the universality of sin. As the apostle states in Romans 3:20, "For no human being will be justified in his sight by works of the law, since through the law comes knowledge of sin." The more one understands who God is and what he is like--the more clearly will he realize his sin and his need for cleansing before God. When we look at human history as a whole or when we look at the human race as a whole, we see that though God has graciously revealed himself and lovingly stretched out his arms--many have not heeded--many have not responded.

The sin of people is underscored in the fact that so often phony substitutes are embraced while the real thing is disdained. Many prefer false religion to the true religion. People seek to satisfy their appetites apart from the will and purpose of God. As a result they remain hungry and spiritually unfulfilled. God loves all, but many do not respond to his love appropriately. We have the commandment that we ought to love our neighbors as ourselves, but we fail to do that. God gives us his commandments, which are good and right for us, and we break them. If we carefully consider the Ten Commandments everyone must recognize that either in an outward act or in intent or thought and desire of the heart, each person has broken all ten of the commandments. No one is excepted; all are in need of God's saving grace, all are in need of the cross of Jesus Christ. All need to affirm in the Communion Service the broken body of Christ and his blood poured out for unworthy sinners on the cross. We need his forgiveness. We need his salvation.

People are not capable of saving themselves. If one looks at all religions other than Christianity--if one surveys the various philosophies--if one consults the opinion of the man on the street--it becomes quite apparent that there are substantial conflicting views as to the nature of God. There is no consensus whether or not he cares about people, whether or not one can have a relationship with him, and if a person can have a meaningful relationship with him--how that relationship can be achieved. We should be grateful that the scriptures tell us clearly about God. They plainly diagnose our sinful condition, and give the good news of salvation and redemption.

Some people seek religious enlightenment, but it is not enough to be enlightened. Of course, correct understanding is to be preferred to ignorance or to misunderstanding. But correct knowledge, at best, is only half of the battle. Then one must embrace it. He must live by it. Not infrequently a person will go to a psychiatrist or a psychologist or some other kind of counselor for therapy. When one talks to them afterward they may relate how much insight they have gained--how they have been enlightened. Now, I do not want to disparage that process. It can be helpful. But enlightenment in and of itself does not save. People have been gaining enlightenment for at least the last six thousand years. In spite of that we see little progress in resolving the macroproblems of humanity, and our personal problems (ultimately rooted in our sin) remain all too vexing and perplexing.

Nor will we be saved by human attempts at moral and ethical behavior. All of the moralisms, all of the lectures on ethics have not delivered us from violence, from lust, from oppression, from all the wickedness and all the unkindnesses that human beings perpetrate upon others. Many people, I am sure, will try to do their best. That is certainly an improvement over indifference or resignation, or (even worse) active participation in wrongdoing. But when the prophets and the apostles look at God, at his holiness, his greatness, his magnificence, the wonder of God--and then they look at humanity--they say that our righteousness is as filthy rags in comparison. We simply do not make it.

Several years ago my wife and I were given a trip to Hawaii by our church in San Jose. Upon arriving in Hawaii, I was determined that I was not going to get sunburned. I knew that it was very easy to get sunburned in that latitude. So when I was not actually in the water I was careful to wear a tee shirt and a hat and to generally protect my body from the Sun. One afternoon I was sitting out on the beach reading a book in the shade of a palm tree. I was being careful. Indeed, I was doing my best! But there was one area that I did not notice. My feet were not in the shade. That evening I had two very red and extremely uncomfortable feet. To put shoes on those feet was out of the question for a day or two. I was doing my best. My heart was in the right place. But my good intentions did not save my feet! I still came up short. The Bible makes it plain that our good intentions will not deliver us. "All have sinned." "There is none righteous, no not one." James wrote, "For whoever keeps the whole law, but fails in one point has become guilty of all of it." [James 2:10] Further, the world is in a mess. I have mentioned some of the perplexing and grievous human problems in previous chapters. Malcolm Muggeridge, Helmut Thielicke, Reinhold Niebuhr, Alexander Solzhenitsyn, and Charles Colson, among others, have done an excellent job of describing the extremely serious predicaments of mankind.

Even the church of Jesus Christ is considerably less than perfect, is it not? All you need to do is to talk to a somewhat informed unbeliever and he will remind you readily of the failings of the church for the past 1900 years. Certain television evangelists in recent years have reminded us that perfidy among Christians cannot be relegated to the past. The apostle Paul wrote to the Corinthians, "we have this treasure in earthen vessels, to show that the transcendent power belongs to God and not to us."[II

Corinthians 4:7] The more carefully we scrutinize the history of the church the more we must be amazed that the gospel has survived at all. But it does survive. People continue to have the opportunity to know Jesus Christ, to turn from their waywardness and to believe in him. People cannot save themselves. Everyone desperately needs a Savior.

The scriptures make it plain that though God is a loving God, far beyond our ability to express the dimensions of that love--and though his grace is exceedingly bountiful, yet God judges people in their sin. He judges those who reject him. The clear message of scripture from the beginning to the end is that we do not live in an irrational world. Neither do we live in an immoral universe, even though it may seem that way at times.

> But as for me, my feet had almost stumbled, my steps had well nigh slipped. For I was envious of the arrogant when I saw the prosperity of the wicked. For they have no pangs; their bodies are sound and sleek. They are not in trouble as other men are; they are not stricken like other men. Therefore pride is their necklace; violence covers them as a garment. Their eyes swell out with fatness, their hearts overflow with follies. They scoff and speak with malice; loftily they threaten oppression. They set their mouths against the heavens, and their tongue struts through the earth....Behold, these are the wicked; always at ease, they increase in riches. All in vain have I kept my heart clean and washed my hands in innocence.
> [Psalm 73:2-9,12,13]

It may appear that things have gotten out of control, but God's goodness remains, and his righteous and holy purposes will be achieved. God always has and he always will distinguish decisively between good and evil.

> Truly thou does set them in slippery places; thou doest make them fall to ruin. How they are destroyed in a moment, swept away utterly by terrors! They are like a dream when one awakes,...For lo, those who are far from thee shall perish; thou dost put an end to those who are false to thee. [Psalm 73:18-20,27]

There is a cosmic difference between right and wrong. One of the stratagems of the evil one is to attempt to obscure that line of distinction, to deprive people of their capacities of discrimination so that everything is seen in shades of gray, and they become incapable of distinguishing right from wrong. Everything becomes relative. God maintains a steady standard of righteousness. He judges the sin of all.

> He who believes in him is not condemned; he who does not believe is condemned already, because he has not believed in the name of the only Son of God. And this is the judgment, that the light has come into the world, and men loved darkness rather than light, because their deeds were evil. [John 3:18,19]

> He who believes in the Son has eternal life; he who does not obey the Son shall not see life, but the wrath of God rests upon him. [John 3:36]

> But by the same word the heavens and earth that now exist have been stored up for fire, being kept until the day of judgment and destruction of ungodly men.
> [II Peter 3:7]

It makes an ultimate difference whether or not one believes in Jesus Christ. The English author, J.R.R. Tolkien wrote, "It does not do to leave a live dragon out of your calculations if you live near him." Perhaps this is not an apt comparison, but Tolkien gives us something to think about! To live and not acknowledge God--to ignore him and his proper claim upon one's life is folly, and the Bible declares it to be folly.

The good news of salvation is nowhere declared more eloquently than in a few verses in the book of Romans, chapter 3. Under the Old Covenant there was the Tabernacle which was later succeeded by the Temple as the center for worship. It contained an outer court that ordinary people could enter. Inside there was the Holy Place that only the priests could enter and only when properly authorized, prepared, and cleansed. Then there was the Holy of Holies that only the High Priest could enter and he only once a year. In a real sense, Romans 3:21-26 is the Holy of Holies of the gospel. It concisely and marvelously reminds all people of their inadequacy, of their sin, of their need of forgiveness. But it also declares the abundant provision for salvation and forgiveness in Jesus Christ. Every sin is completely forgiven in him. We become just in him. The righteous, good, and moral life that we should have lived--Christ lived for us. His righteousness is imputed (credited) to those who believe in him. The believer literally gets credit from the Heavenly Father for the righteousness of Christ!

The cross of Christ should provoke sorrow in every heart because of sin and wrongdoing. The cross of Christ necessarily reminds us of the fact of the judgment of God, because Jesus, the Son of God, met God's wrath and judgment in our place on the cross.

> For our sake he made him to be sin who knew no sin, so that in him we might become the righteousness of God.
> [II Corinthians 5:21]

As II Corinthians 5:21 and Romans 3:21-26 affirm, the cross of Jesus proclaims God's righteousness. It vindicates the holiness and the moral goodness of God. The terrible pain and suffering of Jesus on the cross reminds us of how holy God is, of how severe his judgment is upon sin. But it also teaches us of his grace, and of the great hope that we have through his Son. The cross shows God's mercy; God's love. Salvation is by faith. It is not by works. Good works are appropriate for the person who affirms belief in Jesus Christ, but they are a fruit or product of salvation not the cause of salvation.

This doctrine of grace should not lead into antinomianism, one of the heresies that appeared early in the history of the church. Antinomians placed such an emphasis on grace that obedience to Christ became irrelevant. It ceased to matter what one did, how he lived, or how he treated anyone else. The Bible emphasizes the importance of works. Works are appropriate for the person who has already experienced the grace of God via the cross of Jesus Christ. They then become an expression of one's response to God. But works are not a way to climb a ladder into heaven. Neither are they a means of meriting God's favor. Good works are an appropriate vehicle to express the reality of the grace of God in a Christian's life. Grace and works are compatible. New life in

Christ is solely by faith through grace, but good works are the evidence of the vitality of Christian life.

Salvation is by faith alone.

> Therefore, since we are justified by faith, we have peace with God through our Lord Jesus Christ. [Romans 5:1] There is therefore now no condemnation for those who are in Christ Jesus. [Romans 8:1]

It isn't that Jesus did four-fifths of the task, and the other fifth remains for us to do. He did it all. "Believe in the Lord Jesus and you will be saved."

> "If we confess our sins, he is faithful and just, and will forgive our sins and cleanse us from all unrighteousness."
> [I John 1:9]

Sins are forgiven in Christ Jesus. The believer is accepted into the family of God on the merit of Jesus Christ. Bishop Fulton J. Sheen wrote:

> We want to be saved, but not from our sins ... We are willing to be saved from poverty, from war, from ignorance, from disease, from economic insecurity; such types of salvation leave our individual whims and passions and concupiscences untouched.

Martin Luther said, "There is no greater arrogance than not to desire to be justified by faith in Christ."

When Jesus found a man who had been paralyzed for thirty-eight years lying on one of the porches near the pool of Bethzatha, he asked him, "Do you want to be healed?" There was not any question about the man's need. Neither was there any question about Jesus' power to heal this man. The question had to do with what the man wanted. Did he want to remain where he was? Had he grown so accustomed to his sickness that he was comfortable with it? Or did he indeed want to be healed?

Salvation in Jesus Christ

Salvation is more than knowing that Jesus Christ can forgive and heal and renew. It means a personal commitment of faith to him. Praise God for the good news! We don't have to bring anything with us. We don't have to have any credentials. We don't have to show God what we have done to be worthy of him. We have but to trust in Christ. There is a difference between believing in the structural integrity of a bridge and walking on it. There is a difference between believing in the reliability of an airplane and actually purchasing a ticket and getting on board. There is a difference between believing that an orange is a good fruit and eating an orange and enjoying its taste and benefiting from its nourishment. There is a difference between believing in the saving capability of Christ and by faith entrusting one's self to him.

> Because, if you confess with your lips that Jesus is Lord and believe in your heart that God raised him from the dead, you will be saved. For man believes with his heart and so is justified, and he confesses with his lips and so is saved. [Romans 10:9,10]
>
> I have been crucified with Christ; it is no longer I who live, but Christ who lives in me; and the life I now live in the flesh I live by faith in the Son of God, who loved me and gave himself for me. [Galatians 2:20]
>
> And it shall be that whoever calls upon the name of the Lord shall be saved. [Acts 2:21]
>
> Repent and be baptized every one of you in the name of Jesus Christ for the forgiveness of your sins; and you shall received the gift of the Holy Spirit. [Acts 2:38]

Further Reading

Graham, Billy, *Peace With God*

For Reflection or Discussion

1. In what sense is salvation past, present, and future?

2. What is the most important aspect of salvation for you?

3. What verse or passage in the Bible best expresses salvation to you?

4. Why don't more people believe in Jesus Christ?

5. What arguments can be given against antinomianism?

CHAPTER EIGHT

THE RESURRECTION OF JESUS CHRIST

> But the angel said to the woman, "Do not be afraid; for I know that you seek Jesus who was crucified. He is not here; for he has risen, as he said." [Matthew 28:5,6]

In the events surrounding the arrest, trial, execution, and death of Jesus, two of the bravest people were Joseph of Aramathia and Nicodemus, a Pharisee. These two men were important, wealthy, and powerful. They were members of the Sanhedrin, the governing council of Israel that had condemned Jesus to death. But they had dissented from that flagrantly unjust decision. Jesus had been crucified. His death had been certified to Pilate by the centurion in charge of the crucifixion. The leaders of the Jews, who had sought Jesus' death, never doubted that he was dead. Now that Jesus was dead, his body was taken from the cross. Joseph of Arimathea and Nicodemus courageously went to Pontius Pilate and requested the body of Jesus that they might respectfully bury him. Pilate granted their request.

With love and reverence they wrapped the body of Jesus in linen cloths with spices, and they laid him in a new rock hewn tomb. Then a great stone was rolled against the tomb, and it was sealed by Roman authority. When the leaders of the Sanhedrin ascertained the burial place of Jesus, they came to Pontius Pilate and asked that a guard be set before the tomb. They said, in effect, "We remember while this man lived he said that after he was killed he would rise from the dead, and we don't want to risk his disciples coming and stealing his body. We want to make sure that he remains in the tomb." Pilate granted them a guard of Roman soldiers, and the tomb was sealed. Jesus had predicted, on a number of occasions, that he would rise from the dead. But these predictions were not fully grasped by his disciples. They believed him to be the Messiah, but they had not at that time integrated into their thinking how it was possible for the Messiah to die. While they had retained those teachings, they had not resolved them. But the enemies of Jesus remembered that he had said that he would rise from the dead.

The gospel of John records that early in the ministry of Jesus, the Jews had said to him, "What sign have you to show us for doing this." Jesus answered them, "Destroy this temple, and in three days I will raise it up." [John 2:19] John explains that the initial understanding of these Jews was that Jesus was talking about the magnificent temple which Herod had built, but Jesus was speaking of the temple of his body. We read in Matthew 17:22,23 (later in Jesus' ministry), as Jesus and his disciples were gathering in Galilee, Jesus said,

> The Son of man is to be delivered into the hands of men, and they will kill him, and he will be raised on the third day. [Matthew 17:22,23]

Throughout his ministry there were many occasions when either directly or by implication Jesus spoke of his resurrection. One of the most significant of these predictions is found in Matthew, chapter 12, where Jesus responds to some scribes and Pharisees who asked Jesus for a sign. Whether they believed or not, they knew that many miracles had been attributed to Jesus. They were asking for a more dramatic display of divine power. Jesus rebuked them, because the evidence was quite sufficient if they had the heart to believe. Nonetheless he told them that a great sign would be given:

> For as Jonah was three days and three nights in the belly of the whale, so will the Son of man be three days and three nights in the heart of the earth. [Matthew 12:40]

It is not possible to maintain a credible Christianity without the resurrection. It is the keystone. Remove the resurrection and the entire edifice collapses. The apostle said it well in I Corinthians,

> But if there is no resurrection of the dead, then Christ has not been raised; if Christ has not been raised, then our preaching is in vain and your faith is in vain.
> [I Corinthians 15:13,14]

It is neither wise nor necessary to set faith in opposition to reason and evidence. Of course, there are times when our faith in Christ and our belief in the word of God will outstrip our knowledge and philosophical capacities. Faith in Christ is essential. And, at times, we believe in him and we follow him although many others are going another way.

> for the gate is wide and the way is easy, that leads to destruction, and those who enter by it are many. [Matthew 7:13]

Jesus appealed to the evidence of his own resurrection as verification that God the Father was with him--that he did the work of the Father, and indeed, that the promises that he made were valid promises.

Christianity is an incarnational religion. The realm of God, to be sure, is different--distinct--separate--from the realm in which we live. In the words of Mortimer Adler,

> Heaven being the dwelling place of God, preeminently a purely spiritual being, it cannot be regarded as a physical place, a space that can be occupied by [physical] bodies. It is not out there or up there or anywhere that has a location in the physical cosmos.   [Adler, The Angels and Us, p. 37]

God's ways are not our ways. His thoughts are not our thoughts. As the heavens are high above the earth, so are the ways and thoughts of God above those of people. Nonetheless, there is a connectedness. God speaks to us. He spoke to Abraham and Isaac and Jacob. He revealed himself to Moses. He declared himself to the people of Israel. And he became human.

There is a relationship between heaven and earth; between this life and the life to come. Just as we err if we totally merge God with his creation and become pantheists (so that everything is divine)--we also err if we so emphasize the transcendence of God so that there is no possible connection between him and people. If that were so, we could not know God. We should be people without hope. But our belief in Christ is well founded. Jesus Christ lived and died among people, and his resurrection is the cornerstone of faith in him.

The Bible, then, teaches plainly that Jesus was dead. There have been some (especially in the twentieth century) who have contended that Jesus never really died. Such specious explanations usually claim that he simply fainted and, later on in the coldness of the tomb, he revived. One of several difficulties with theories like that is the inability to give an adequate explanation of how Jesus got out of the tomb. Neither do they offer a plausible explanation of what he did when he escaped from the tomb or when he died and where he was subsequently buried. Did Jesus revive after at least thirty-six hours in a cold tomb? Did he then unwrap himself from the grave clothes and spices with which he was bound? Did he roll the stone from the tomb, and somehow convince the Roman guard that they were to allow him to go free? The scriptures accurately assert that Jesus was dead!

Let us briefly consider Jesus' experiences leading up to the crucifixion. He was received into Jerusalem on Palm Sunday with a tumultuous welcome. During the following week, every day, all day long, he taught in the temple. For a period of five days he ministered intensively to large groups and small groups and individuals. Those who have experienced ministry to people for long hours know how physically and emotionally exhausting that can be. Beyond that, Jesus was under incessant attack from his enemies. The night before he was to be crucified he went without sleep. He was with the disciples at the Last Supper in the Upper Room, where he had washed their feet and where he had engaged in extensive instructions for them. The record of some of these teachings is contained in the gospel of John, chapters 14, 15, and 16.

With his disciples he went out to the Garden of Gethsemane, and there was engaged in intense emotional struggle in prayer to the Heavenly Father. Sometime after midnight his antagonists arrived. He was accosted by a great crowd with swords and clubs. He was arrested, and subjected to a series of trials before the High Priest and the Council--then before the Roman governor, Pontius Pilate, then before Herod Antipas, the ruler of Galilee, and finally again before Pilate.

Pilate ordered Jesus scourged. Many did not survive the terrble bloody beating that was Roman scourging. Jesus suffered further severe physical abuse at the hands of the soldiers. He was so weakened by all of this that he was unable to carry his own cross.

They had to impress a bystander, Simon of Cyrene, to carry the cross. For more than six hours Jesus hung on the cross. It is true, that because of the cruel design of crucifixion the victims could linger and die slowly over a period of as long as two days.

Because they wanted to hasten the death of these particular victims they broke the legs of the thieves who were crucified on either side of Jesus. When their legs were broken they could no longer support themselves, and they died of suffocation. The soldiers came to Jesus and saw that he was already dead--so, they did not break his legs. A soldier thrust a spear in his side, and the Bible bears testimony that the body fluids flowed out. Jesus was dead. Pilate and those who sought his crucifixion were convinced that he was dead. Otherwise Pilate would not have released the body of Jesus. Would those who loved him have made efforts at embalming him, and have placed his body in a tomb had they believed there was any sign, whatsoever, of life in him?

The enemies of Jesus never argued that he did not die. That was not the apologetic of those who sought his crucifixion or of others who disbelieved in him in the first century. Their claim was that the guard had fallen asleep, and that the disciples had come (and rolled away the stone) and taken the body of Jesus and hidden it. Of course, that is an incredible tale! The whole purpose of setting a guard is to insure that a round-the-clock vigil is maintained. And those soldiers certainly knew well what severe punishment awaited guards who were found asleep on duty! Read in Acts, chapter 12, of the execution of the sentries by Herod Agrippa I after Peter was miraculously delivered from prison.

The idea that these disciples, who fled in fear when Jesus was with them, would assault the guard at the tomb, roll back the stone, take away the body of Jesus (whom they dearly loved), hide that body, and then falsely bear testimony to his resurrection is far more difficult to believe than that, indeed, Jesus rose from the dead as the gospels clearly and plainly declare. Simon Greenleaf, professor of law at Harvard University in the last century, wrote the following regarding the disciples:

> They had every possible motive to review carefully the grounds of their faith and the evidences of the great facts and truths which they asserted; and these motives were

pressed upon their attention with the most melancholy and terrific frequency. It was therefore impossible that they could have persisted in affirming the truths they have narrated, had not Jesus actually risen from the dead, and had they not known this fact as certainly as they knew any other fact. If it were morally possible for them to have been deceived in this matter, every human motive operated to lead them to discover and avow their error. To have persisted in so gross a falsehood after it was know to them, was not only to encounter, for life all the evils which man could inflict, from without, but to endure also the pangs of inward and conscious guilt; with no hope of future peace, no testimony of a good conscience, no expectation of honor or esteem among men, no hope of happiness in this life, or in the world to come.

Jesus died. He was entombed. And then on that first Easter Sunday morning, the tomb was found to be empty.

We have in Matthew, chapter 28, the picture of the first witness to the empty tomb. It was the mighty angel, who came down and rolled away the stone, accompanied by an earthquake. We read that his appearance was like lightening and his raiment was as white as snow. Seasoned Roman soldiers became as dead men when they saw that angel, and they fled the scene! When the women arrived, the angel said, "He is not here for he has risen as he said. Come see the place where he lay." Then the women: Mary Magdelene, Mary the mother of James and John, and Joanna bore testimony to the fact that the tomb was empty. Mary Magdalene told Peter and John of the empty tomb. They then ran to the tomb. Because he ran faster John got there first. But John did not enter the tomb until Peter came. Peter entered and John followed him. John bears this marvelous testimony: that when he saw the place where Jesus' body had been, he believed. He saw the grave clothes lying as if the body was still in them. It was as if Jesus had evaporated! This convinced John that the resurrection had taken place.

There were hundreds of witnesses to the resurrection and many resurrection appearances of Jesus over a period of forty days. We read of Jesus' loving appearance to Mary Magdalene in John, chapter 20. She was not expecting to see him, and at first thought that he was the caretaker of the garden. But Jesus made himself known to her. Another of the first persons to see Jesus after he came back from the grave was Simon Peter. Jesus' appearance to Peter is mentioned by those who walked with Jesus on the road to Emmaus (Luke, chapter 24), and in Paul's summary of the resurrection appearances (I Corinthians, chapter 15). Many find that scene of Jesus walking with the two disciples on their way to Emmaus to be especially appealing. At first they did not recognize Jesus. But when he sat down with them and broke the bread and gave thanks, they realized that it was Jesus.

Later on, on that first Sunday, Jesus appeared to most of the disciples (who were sequestered behind locked doors). But Thomas was not with them, and when they told Thomas of the resurrection Thomas said,

> Unless I see in his hands the print of the nails, and place my finger in the mark of the nails, and place my hand in his side, I will not believe. [John 20:25]

Eight days later Jesus appeared to the disciples and Thomas was present. Jesus said to Thomas,

> Put your finger here, and see my hands; and put out your hand and place it in my side; do not be faithless, but believing. [John 20:27]

Thomas acknowledged the reality of the resurrection, responding, "My Lord and my God!".

Sometime after his encounter with Thomas, Jesus appeared to seven of the disciples by the Sea of Galilee. In I Corinthians, chapter 15, the apostle Paul relates that Jesus appeared to his brother, James, and that he appeared to five hundred believers at one time. Paul then testifies, "Last of all as to one untimely born, he appeared also to me." [I Corinthians 15:8] Paul was one of the best educated people of his time. He was a Pharisee, and a zealous opponent of Christianity. His life changed, and he became a convincing witness to the resurrection. The transformation of Saul of Tarsus into Paul, the apostle, is another strong evidence that Jesus was not held by death.

Stephen, one of the first seven deacons, bore his persona witness to the resurrection: "Behold, I see the heavens opened, and the Son of man standing at the right hand of God:" (Acts 7:56). We turn to the book of Revelation, chapter 1, and see that the risen Lord again appears to John the apostle. Boswell, the biographer of the great lexicographer and writer Samuel Johnson, relates a statement by Johnson,

> For revealed religion, there was such historical evidence, as, upon any subject not religious, would have left no doubt. Had the facts recorded in the New Testament been mere civil occurrences, no one would have called in question the testimony by which they are established; [James Boswell, *Life of Samuel Johnson LL.D.*]

Another way of saying what Samuel Johnson said is that most people accept without question many other facts from history with far less evidence than we have for the resurrection.

To review: the argument is made by some that the affirmations of the resurrection were a plot, a subterfuge, or just a mistake. Possibly the disciples thought that they saw Jesus when actually they did not. The refutation of these skeptical arguments is that the resurrection appearances occurred over a period of forty days to different persons under a variety of circumstances. Contrary to their expectations, many were convinced that Jesus had been raised from the dead. Further, with the passage of time, they did not change their minds. They staked their lives to the truth of their witness regarding the resurrection. It is not too much to say that the Christian religion is founded on the resurrection of Jesus Christ, and that its existence is inexplicable without the resurrection.

The New Testament writers affirmed that they spoke the truth. Peter wrote,

> For we did not follow cleverly devised myths when we made known to you the power and coming of our Lord Jesus Christ, but we were eyewitnesses of his majesty.
> [II Peter 1:16]

Peter says, in effect, "I am not giving you hearsay information. I am not telling you something that I have dreamed up. This is not a matter that would be nice to be true if we could believe it. I am telling you what is sure and certain and what I saw with my own eyes. This is the truth if ever I told it!" There is a similar passage in I John,

> That which was from the beginning, which we have heard, which we have seen with our eyes, which we have looked upon and touched with our hands, concerning the word of life--the life was made manifest, and we saw it, and testify to it, and proclaim to you... [I John 1:1,2]

John states plainly that his statements about Jesus Christ come from first hand personal experiences. He knows them to be true. If that is not so, then he is a blatant lier and cruel deceiver, and the New Testament is not worthy of serious attention.

> To them he presented himself alive after his passion by many proofs, appearing to them during forty days, and speaking of the kingdom of God. [Acts 1:3]

Either all of these people were deluded for their entire lifetimes or they were deliberately lying and engaged in one of the most wicked deceptions in all of history or they told the truth. They laid down their lives for their claim that Jesus Christ was raised from the dead. And they bore their initial witness to the resurrection not off in China or away in India. They affirmed the fact of the resurrection in Jerusalem. Jerusalem was the place where Jesus had been publicly crucified. Jerusalem was the site of Jesus burial known to the Jewish and Roman authorities. Jerusalem was the place where the disciples knew very well that Jesus had been raised from the dead. Then in Antioch, in Athens, in Corinth, in Ephesus, in Rome, and throughout the Mediterranean world they proclaimed that Christ had been crucified under the authority of Rome, and that he had been delivered from death by the power of God.

George Eldon Ladd wrote the following in his fine book, *I Believe in the Resurrection of Jesus*,

> If Jesus is not raised, redemptive history ends in the cul de

sac of a Palestinian grave. Then God is not the living God, nor is he the God of the living, as Jesus said. Death is stronger than God. Death is stronger than God's word. God's acts are proven futile in the face of man's greatest enemy, death. One may not discount the resurrection and accept the Bible's witness to redemptive history. As we have said, it is the cornerstone of our faith, but it is a solid and sure cornerstone.

Jesus Christ was raised from the dead. Again and again, not only the first century witnesses (who are certainly truthful, honest, and reliable) but people down through the ages continue to bear witness to the reality of Jesus Christ. The Russia For Christ mission organization produces a monthly newsletter, Freedom. As a result of their broadcasts into the Soviet Union they receive letters from listeners in the USSR. The following is a part of a letter from a young person, who was involved in drugs in the Soviet Union:

> I want to testify to the power of Jesus Christ. I have read how Christ raised a dead man to life. He approached him and said, "Come forth". That was all he needed to do, say the word. No mystical incantations, no incense, no loud music. He just spoke the words. I too was dead. And he called me back to life from the nightmare world of drug addiction. I was unable to help myself. Then Jesus called me. He did so with his word. And that word was my salvation. Before, I always used to say to Christians, "You have nothing but words to back you up." When I was living on drugs I was existing in a psychedelic world of illusion. I realized that the world contained no reality or substance. And now I am being healed by the word of Christ. It was further said that the man whom Christ raised from the dead had been in his grave for four days, and had begun to decompose. People who knew me before would say that I too had been decomposing as so many of us are. Yet Christ did not turn away from the rank oder of corruption but gazes upon us with love and says, "Come forth". He makes no flowery speeches, but what he says is sufficient. It was so for me. I am grateful to God that he showed me the power of Jesus Christ and I want to share this knowledge with the world.

Similar testimony is given over and over again by people who have met Jesus Christ and have found him to be alive!

The truth of the resurrection relegates any other problems to a relatively minor level of importance. If Jesus was raised from the dead, then his word is absolutely reliable, and the Bible is eminently believable. The resurrection demands a response, even if it be the response of disbelief and rejection. It is the supreme event of history. It cannot be treated casually. There are many who believe in the fact of the life of Jesus Christ and in his death and resurrection. But somehow these great truths are trivial to them-- they have no hold upon them. No response is forthcoming. The disciples recognized the truth of the resurrection, and their lives were transformed. The resurrection reveals that the love of God is not just a general sentiment extended to all of his creatures--but that it is a very specific love. He has sent his Son, because he wants people personally to have fellowship with him. Lives are to be changed and transformed by belief in Christ and through the power of the Holy Spirit working in people's lives.

In the resurrection, we have power over death--we see victory. Because of the resurrection of Jesus Christ, we too may look forward to rising from the dead. Because of the resurrection we may be new creatures. This power, which God demonstrated in the resurrection, can change the life of the one who will come to Christ and facilitate the work of God within him. If lives are not changed as a result of the resurrection, then it has not had the significance that it ought to have.

If death is the end--if there is nothing beyond the grave--then, the only matters of importance are the affairs of this life. There is little to be said about how we live except, perhaps, that we live as good animals. If this life is the end, then we would expect people to live as if it were the end. But if this life is not the end, if the resurrection has opened up a whole new vista, then the way that we live our lives ought to be transformed.

Sometimes the sweetest victories follow defeat. Because the crucifixion was such an awful thing, the resurrection was so much more glorious. The resurrection was a tremendous victory. It means that those who had beaten, spit upon, and mocked Jesus had been wrong. The iniquitous plot to blot out the life of the perfect man had failed. It proved that the grave need not be a dismal defeat, but that there is a far better life. If the resurrection is true, than the Bible is true. If the resurrection never occurred, then the Bible is false. The church is not a tombstone, but a living monument to one who is alive! The great theologian, John Calvin, eloquently expressed the implications of the resurrection:

> For how was it possible for him by dying to liberate us from death, if he had himself remained under its power? How could he have obtained the victory for us, if he had been vanquished in the contest? Wherefore we ascribe our salvation partly to the death of Christ, and partly to his resurrection; we believe that sin was abolished and death destroyed by the former; that righteousness was restored and life established by the latter; yet so that the former discovers its power and efficacy in us by means of the latter. [Calvin, *Institutes of the Christian Religion*, II, XVI, XIII]

Further Reading

Ladd, George Eldon, *I Believe in the Resurrection of Jesus*, Wm. B. Eerdmans Publishing Co.
Morrison, Frank, *Who Moved The Stone?*, Zondervan Publishing House
Shannon, Foster, *God Is Light*, Chapter 7, Green Leaf Press
Smith, Wilbur, *Therefore Stand*, Chapter VIII, W.A. Wilde Co.

For Reflection or Discussion

1. What are some of the strongest assurances or evidences for you that Jesus Christ rose from the dead?

2. If the resurrection is true, what are the most significant implications for the one who believes in Jesus Christ?

3. Why do sceptics attack other biblical claims or miracles relatively more frequently than they attack the resurrection?

CHAPTER NINE

THE HOLY SPIRIT

While there is greater emphasis on the Holy Spirit in the New Testament, references to the Holy Spirit are found throughout the Bible. The second verse in the Bible reads, "and the Spirit of God was moving over the face of the waters." The Holy Spirit comes upon many individuals in the Old Testament to accomplish specific works. The Spirit of God gave Samson leadership ability and enormous physical strength, and God gave deliverance through Samson to the people of Israel from the oppression of the Philistines. The Spirit of God came upon king Saul so that he prophesied. Yet later in his life Saul was aware that the Spirit was no longer with him. David prayed that God would not take his Holy Spirit from him. Surely the Holy Spirit was at work in the ministries of all of the prophets. Nonetheless, the doctrine of the Holy Spirit receives fuller and more complete emphasis in the New Testament. It is as if the Holy Spirit was operating back stage during the Old Covenant--but under the New Covenant (especially beginning with Pentecost) he has come on center stage.

Luther, Melanchthon, Zwingli, Calvin, Knox, and other prominent leaders involved at the outset of the Protestant Reformation had two major doctrinal concerns: soteriology and ecclesiology. Soteriology has to do with the means whereby a person comes into a vital relationship with God. What does it mean to believe in Christ? Is salvation solely on the basis of faith? If works are important, in what way are they properly associated with salvation? The second great issue was ecclesiology, the doctrine of the church. Prior to the Reformation the church at Rome had claimed to be the church in all of Europe, if not in the world. The nature of the church was, therefore, of great concern to the Reformers. Could the church be properly constituted only by bishops authorized by the Church of Rome? Or were there legitimate New Testament criterion whereby Protestants and their ministers could be recognized as a legitimate part of the church?

An extremely important benefit derived from the eruption of the Protestant Reformation is that many today have a solid grasp of the doctrine of salvation by grace. We understand that people come into relationship with God solely on the basis of the perfect atoning work of Jesus Christ. We are quite clear that a person cannot merit God's favor or earn his salvation! We should also have a better understanding of the nature of the church: that it is composed of all who are gathered to worship God, to celebrate the sacraments, and to share the good news under a system of church order that is compatible with the scriptures.

Because of these necessary major concerns of the Protestant Reformers, beginning in the sixteenth century, the biblical teachings on the Holy Spirit were frequently underemphasized and sometimes outright neglected. They were not denied, but inadequate attention was paid to them. At least, in part, due to the insufficient attention given to the Holy Spirit in much of Protestantism, the Pentecostal movement developed in the late 1800s and early 1900s. On the whole that movement has provided a healthy corrective influence for much of Protestantism regarding important truths about the Holy Spirit. A benefit of that influence is that the church as a whole has become more aware of the work of the Holy Spirit and his manifold ministries. An unfortunate result has been the tendency to too closely connect the gift of speaking in tongues as an exclusive sign of the reality and activity of the Holy Spirit.

Most Christian movements fall victim to emphasizing one biblical truth at the expense of other significant biblical truths. In many contemporary charismatic groups there has been a disproportionate emphasis on the Holy Spirit to the neglect of other important biblical doctrines. What follows is an attempt to set forth what I believe to be the central biblical truths regarding the Holy Spirit from the Bible:

I. THE PRESENCE AND WORK OF THE HOLY SPIRIT IS VITALLY IMPORTANT TO EVERY CHRISTIAN

1. *The Christian believer is born of the Spirit.* It is by the Spirit of God that a person is inclined to believe in Jesus Christ. Jesus said, "No one can come to me unless the Father who sent me draws him:" (John 6:44). If one connects this statement with the first half of John, chapter three, it is plain that it is by the Holy Spirit that one is inclined toward God and, thus, is born of the Spirit of God. Jesus stated in John 16:8,

> And when he (the Holy Spirit) comes, he will convince the world concerning sin and righteousness and judgment;

The Holy Spirit

It is by the Spirit of God that one becomes a member of the Christian family (by means of the new birth). Jesus said to Nicodemus,

> Truly, truly, I say to you, unless one is born of water and the Spirit, he cannot enter the kingdom of God. That which is born of the flesh is flesh, and that which is born of the Spirit is spirit. [John 3:5,6]

To this religious leader, Jesus emphasized that it is by spiritual birth that people enter the kingdom of God. Thus, we read in Titus 3:5,6,

> he saved us, not because of deeds done by us in righteousness, but in virtue of his own mercy, by the washing of regeneration and renewal in the Holy Spirit, which he poured out upon us richly through Jesus Christ our Savior,

2. *The Christian believer is instructed by the Spirit.* Some of the richest teachings on the Holy Spirit are found in the gospel of John, chapters fourteen, fifteen, and sixteen. Foreseeing his departure from earth and his return to be with the Father in heaven, Jesus especially emphasized the teaching ministry of the Holy Spirit:

> But the Counselor, the Holy Spirit, whom the Father will send in my name, he will teach you all things, and bring to your remembrance all that I have said to you.
> [I John 14:26]

This instructional ministry by the Spirit of God is emphasized in I Corinthians, chapter two:

> Now we have received not the spirit of the world, but the Spirit which is from God, that we might understand the gifts bestowed on us by God. And we impart this in words not taught by human wisdom but taught by the Spirit, interpreting spiritual truths to those who possess the Spirit.

II Peter 1:21 also emphasizes the instruction of the Holy Spirit, no prophecy ever came by the impulse of man, but men moved by theHoly Spirit spoke from God.

3. *The Christian is strengthened by the Spirit.* Recall Jesus' famous command in Acts, chapter one,

> But you shall receive power when the Holy Spirit has come upon you.

The effect of this promise of Jesus is seen in Acts 4:31 (and in many other places),

> And when they had prayed, the place in which they were gathered together was shaken; and they were all filled with the Holy Spirit and spoke the word of God with boldness.

The apostle Paul emphasized the strengthening of the Spirit in Romans 15:13,

> May the God of hope fill you with all joy and peace in believing, so that by the power of the Holy Spirit you may abound in hope.

The teachings of the Bible, especially the New Testament, on the Holy Spirit are substantial. This is not a doctrine to be neglected. The ministry of the Holy Spirit is important to every person, inclining us toward Christ, enabling our spiritual birth, instructing us in God's truths and giving us power and boldness to follow Christ and bear witness for him.

II. EVERYONE WHO BELIEVES IN JESUS CHRIST RECEIVES NEW BIRTH THROUGH THE HOLY SPIRIT AND IS INDWELT BY THE HOLY SPIRIT

The New Testament clearly teaches that everyone who believes in Jesus Christ is both born of the Holy Spirit and indwelt by the Spirit of God. In the new birth one is drawn to Christ, convicted of his sin, turns from his sin, places his faith and trust in Jesus Christ, and is associated with the people of God. This is the perspective of the inquirer or believer. The other side is the activity of God through his Spirit. Thus, if one believes in Christ, it is because spiritual life has been imparted to him by the Holy Spirit.

The Holy Spirit

God takes up residence and lives in the person who has been born anew.

> Guard the truth that has been entrusted to you by the Holy Spirit who dwells within us. [II Timothy 1:14]

In writing the above words, the apostle states a common truth for all Christians: the Holy Spirit dwells within the believer. In both First and Second Corinthians he emphasized their common possession of the Holy Spirit. That living presence of the Holy Spirit in their lives was not dependent upon their spiritual maturity, because of all of the churches we read of in the letters in the New Testament--the church at Corinth was the most spiritually immature. There were divisions among them. They had moral problems. They were misusing the gifts of the Spirit. It is apparent that the indwelling of the Holy Spirit in the Christian does not depend upon his level of spiritual maturity, although everyone should certainly aspire to spiritual maturity. Thus, the apostle wrote to the Corinthians appealing to them to move from disunity to unity and from disobedience to obedience. The very foundation of that appeal was that the Holy Spirit was already at work within their lives.

> Do you not know that you are God's temple and that God's Spirit dwells in you? [I Corinthians 3:16]

> Do you not know that your body is a temple of the Holy Spirit within you, which you have from God? [I Corinthians 6:19]

> For we are the temple of the living God; as God said, "I will live in them and move among them, and I will be their God, and they shall be my people. [II Corinthians 6:16]

The scriptures assure the Christian that the Holy Spirit dwells within him.

It has become much more common in recent years, especially since the advent of Jimmy Carter as President to refer to "born again" Christians. I think this is intended to indicate a person whose life has been radically and dramatically changed by Jesus Christ; a person who has come to know Jesus Christ in a very definite way, as, perhaps, contrasted with people who have come to

Christ gradually or from childhood. I have no quarrel with people who use the terminology "born again Christian". It can, on occasion, be a useful designation. However, if that terminology causes people to think that there are two kinds of Christians, those who are born again and those who are not, then we are encouraging erroneous thinking. All who truly believe in Christ have been born anew of the Holy Spirit.

The particular ways or processes by which they have come to Christ may vary. But most basic to their belief in Christ, is the work of the Holy Spirit in their hearts. The story is told of two men who were blind and deaf and asleep on the railroad tracks. At the very last moment a stranger dragged them from the tracks to avoid their destruction by an oncoming train. When the men realized their narrow escape and their deliverance, one leaped for joy in emotional celebration. The other knelt in quiet gratitude to God overwhelmed by the mercy of God. Both were saved, but their response to their deliverance was markedly different. Similarly the individual's response to being saved by Jesus Christ may be quite different--but genuine.

In some quarters, it has become customary to refer to "Spirit filled Christians". In all fairness, this is biblical terminology. The first seven deacons were to be men who were full of the Spirit (Acts, chapter six). It was said of Barnabas, the associate of the apostle Paul, that he was a man full of the Spirit. But we can take what is essentially biblical terminology, and it can be misused and misunderstanding can result. Again we must beware of thinking that there are two classes of Christian: "born again Christians" and "not born again Christians". If one is not born again and does not have the Spirit of God, then he is not a Christian! If one does believe in Jesus Christ then it is because he has been born, anew and his body has become a temple of the Holy Spirit.

Let me ask you a question. If you believe in Jesus Christ, how do you know that you are forgiven of your sins? Is it not on the authority of the scriptures? For example, we read in I John 1:9, "If we confess our sins, he is faithful and just, and will forgive us our sins..." It is because we trust God's word that we can know that our sins are forgiven. If you believe in Jesus Christ how do you know that you are a member of the family of God? Is it not because God has gone on record in the Bible? Jesus said, "him who comes to me I will not cast out." [John 6:37] The Bible

The Holy Spirit

declares that whosoever will believe may come to Christ; that if we believe in him with our hearts and confess him with our mouths we are saved (Romans 10:9,10). This all is on the authority of the word of God! It is on that same authority that the believer knows that God, the Holy Spirit, is living within him!

III. IS THERE SOMETHING MORE?

Having affirmed the importance of the ministry and the indwelling of the Holy Spirit in everyone who believes--perhaps, this is the point to inquire, is there something more? Can one have a second filling of the Spirit? Can one have additional experiences with the Spirit? Are there blessings from the Spirit that come as a result of further spiritual growth or deeper commitment? The New Testament surely indicates an increase in the blessings of the Holy Spirit for the Christian who will seek a greater fulness of the Spirit.

Let us again refer to the event of Pentecost described in Acts, chapter two. This was in fulfillment of the promise of Christ to the disciples that upon his departure from earth, God would send the Holy Spirit to be with them. There was a tremendous sound. There were visible signs, and as a result of that dramatic infilling of the Holy Spirit they were enabled to communicate the gospel to people in many languages. Jews had come to Jerusalem for the great Jewish feast of Pentecost from Parthia, from Cappadocia, Elam, Rome, Egypt, Libya, Crete, and other distant places. Being native to those areas, many of them spoke only the language of the locale where they had been reared. Undoubtedly many of them did not understand the Hebrew or Aramaic of Judea. During that Pentecost festival each one heard the gospel proclaimed in his native tongue from the mouths of the apostles.

Presumably, before the day of Pentecost the disciples were already believers in Christ. I do not think there are many people who would say that Pentecost was a conversion experience for them They had previously confessed Jesus as Messiah. They had been with Jesus for at least three years. It is inconceivable that Jesus would have said, "I will give you the keys of the kingdom of heaven", if they were all unsaved! They came to the Pentecost event as believers. Therefore, with the example of the day of Pentecost, it is reasonable to deduce that there are additional things that the Holy Spirit can do with and for the believer.

However, we must take care that we do not push that principle too hard. Pentecost was a very special event. It was the assurance--the sign that the promises of Christ to his disciples regarding the advent of the Holy Spirit had been fulfilled.

There are not many, even in the Pentecostal family of churches, who insist on the rushing of a mighty wind and visible signs and the ability to speak in foreign tongues as a sign of the presence of the Holy Spirit. These were special signs. The manifestation of these signs are recorded on three more occasions in the book of Acts. Each occurrence was for a very specific purpose:

1. Acts, chapter eight, when the gospel was first preached in Samaria, and Peter and John were sent to Samaria by the church in Jerusalem. There were signs similar to those of the day of Pentecost confirming to Peter and John that those Samaritan believers had received the Holy Spirit. I believe that it had been confirmed in the minds of the Christians in Jerusalem that Jews, who by faith believed in Jesus as the Messiah, could receive the gift of the Holy Spirit, but they may not have been so sure about Samaritans and perhaps even less sure about Gentiles!

2. Acts, chapter ten, the conversion of the Roman centurion Cornelius. He and his household believed, and again there were signs similar to those on Pentecost in Jerusalem. In fact, if you read that passage, if it had not been for those signs it would have been extremely difficult for the Jewish Christian church to acknowledge that Gentiles could come directly to Christ without also establishing themselves as Jews. Peter's argument to the Christian community in Jerusalem (Acts 11:1-18) was that Cornelius and his household received the Holy Spirit just as the disciples had, and, therefore, they must be recognized as fellow believers.

3. The final time that the manifestation of these very special signs is mentioned is in Acts, chapter nineteen, regarding certain believers in Ephesus. The first occurrence at Pentecost was to confirm to the church that the promises of Christ regarding the Holy Spirit had been fulfilled. The demonstrations in Samaria and at Caesarea were to indicate the inclusiveness of the gospel. Their occurrence at Ephesus demonstrated that even at the distance of a thousand miles from Jerusalem the same God was at work among those who would receive him, whether Jew or Gentile.

The Holy Spirit

There is a further point to be make in this regard from Hebrews, chapter two:

> Therefore, we must pay the closer attention to what we have heard, lest we drift away from it. For if the message declared by angels was valid and every transgression or disobedience received a just retribution, how shall we escape if we neglect such a great salvation? It was declared at first by the Lord, and it was attested to us by those who heard him, while God also bore witness by signs and wonders and various miracles and by *gifts of the Holy Spirit distributed according to his own will.* [Hebrews 2:1-4]

The writer to the Hebrews is contending for the importance of responding to the gospel of Christ. He affirms that one should respond to the gospel because it has been spoken by the Lord himself--because it has been reaffirmed by the apostles--and because special signs and miracles were associated with that initial proclamation of the gospel. The clear implication of this passage is that those were unique signs. The visual manifestations, a sound like the rushing of a mighty wind, and the enabling of the disciples to speak in foreign languages were distinct and unusual even to the believing community of the first century. If they were not a special sign why should the writer to the Hebrews refer to them as extraordinary evidence that one should respond to the gospel and believe in Jesus Christ?

There are those today who would associate the filling of the Spirit with a single spiritual gift, speaking in tongues. The Bible speaks of being filled with the Spirit, but it does not necessarily associate that filling with speaking in tongues.

> But be filled with the Spirit, addressing one another in psalms and hymns and spiritual songs, singing and making melody to the Lord with all your heart, always and for everything giving thanks in the name of the Lord Jesus Christ to God the Father. [Ephesians 5:18-20]

This is the only passage in the New Testament that commands one to be filled with the Spirit of God. Being filled with the Spirit clearly implies something in addition to believing in Christ. And it, therefore, means more than being born of the Spirit. We can use the analogy of a great electric generator that transmits power to farms, factories, offices, and homes. There is no question about the power produced by the generator. It has been rated by competent engineers and his demonstrated its ability to produce electrical power day after day. The problem has to do with the capacity of the transmission lines. The greater the capacity of the lines--the greater the potential flow of electricity. Factories using enormous amounts of electrical energy have great transmission cables coming into them. But if we were to attempt to get such enormous power into a private residence--it would blow out all of the systems.

The Christian should surely expect to grow in his ability to receive the presence and power of the Holy Spirit! It is a reasonable inference from the New Testament that a person can increase his receptivity to the ministry of the Spirit of God. There is no Christian who cannot be more fully used of God than is the case at present. Every believer should expect to grow in openness to the Spirit of God. We are to be filled with the Spirit! Interestingly, in this passage from Ephesians the marks of being filled with the Spirit are music and thanksgiving rather than speaking in tongues.

> "Singing and making melody to the Lord with all your heart, and always and for everything giving thanks,".
> [Ephesians 5:19,20]

The singing of Christian music can be a powerful instrumentality of the Holy Spirit.

We read in Acts 4:8 that the apostle Peter was filled with the Holy Spirit and the result (in Acts 4:13) was that others took note of his boldness and that of John as well. We find the same effect in Acts 4:31: boldness is a result of being filled with the Holy Spirit. Stephen, the first Christian martyr (after Jesus) had a vision of heaven as a result of being filled with the Holy Spirit.

> But he, full of the Holy Spirit, gazed into heaven and saw the glory of God, and Jesus standing at the right hand of God; [Acts 8:55]

It was said of Barnabas, who was noted for his generosity, that he was a man filled with the Spirit. If one is to look for further evidences that point toward greater filling with the Spirit, he should carefully consider the fruit of the Spirit listed in Galatians 5:22,23: "love, joy, peace, longsuffering, gentleness, goodness, faith, meekness temperance."

The book of I John emphasizes that love for Christ comes first. John aligns love for Christ with the ministry of the Spirit. In I Corinthians, chapter twelve, we find two lists of spiritual gifts. In Romans, chapter twelve, another list of spiritual gifts, and in Ephesians, chapter four, a shorter list. If one follows the reasoning of the apostle Paul in I Corinthians, chapter twelve, he teaches that the Spirit gives gifts to the body of Christ for its well-being and upbuilding, and that there are a diversity of gifts. There are gifts of prophesying (the ability to effectively declare the word of God), of teaching; of administration; of being helpful; of liberality; and of speaking in tongues--among others.

I Corinthians, chapter twelve, states that the gifts of the Spirit can be compared to the various parts of the human body; e.g. the hands and the feet and the eyes and the ears. The apostle asks the rhetorical question, "is the whole body an eye?" The conclusion is obvious. If the whole body were an eye there would be no means of locomotion or digestion or circulation or thought. It is the different parts that make the whole . The clear implication is that everyone is not going to have the gift of preaching or of teaching or of administration. Neither is everyone going to have the gift of speaking in tongues. The gifts are given as God apportions them for the strengthening and upbuilding of his church. It is unfortunate that on occasion undue emphasis is given to one of the gifts, because there are many gifts and each one is important. In the four lists in the New Testament, the gift of speaking in tongues is mentioned twice. In two of the lists it is not mentioned at all. When people single out a particular gift and exalt it over and above the others they do exactly what I Corinthians 12:14-27 says should not be done.

The possession of a spiritual gift is not in and of itself a sign of spiritual maturity. A person may have the gift of prophesying (preaching: declaring the word of God), but the possession of that gift does not give assurance that that individual will be spiritually mature. Similarly one may have the gift of being a teacher or an administrator, but we cannot thereby assume a spiritually mature person. And it is a delusion for people to think that because they have the gift of speaking in tongues they are spiritually mature!

They may or they may not be. The spiritual gift that God gives to an individual for his benefit and, hopefully, for the upbuilding of the church is not for the division of the church. So the gifts are given by God as it pleases him. Every Christian should seek the fulness of the Spirit. All should seek to grow in the Spirit. Every believer should seek to exercise as well as he can every gift that God has given to him. But there should be a mutuality of respect--a recognition that all do not possess every gift--but that each spiritual gift is important to the church.

I Corinthians, chapter thirteen, is the "love chapter". It is a commentary on the Christian's use of God-given spiritual gifts. It declares that the overriding criterion is to be that of love. It is unfortunate that sometimes the connection between I Corinthians chapter thirteen and chapter twelve which precedes it and chapter fourteen which follows it are not clearly seen. In the development of the doctrine of spiritual gifts these three chapters are inseparable.

> Love is patient and kind; love is not jealous or boastful; it is not arrogant or rude. Love does not insist on its own way; it is not irritable or resentful; it does not rejoice at wrong, but rejoices in the right. Love bears all things, believes all things, hopes all things, endures all things.
> [I Corinthians 13:4-7]

This is the deliberate commentary of the Bible on the use of spiritual gifts. May we always be guided by it!

For Reflection or Discussion

1. What is the most important ministry of the Holy Spirit to every Christian?

2. What is one of the surest signs of "spirituality"?

3. What can a person do to encourage the work of the Holy Spirit in his life?

4. What is the difference between spiritual gifts and the "fruit of the Spirit"?

CHAPTER TEN
PRAYER

The Bible emphasizes the centrality of prayer. It specifically commands those who believe in God to pray, and in a variety of ways it commends prayer. In the Sermon on the Mount, Jesus gave instructions in regard to prayer (Matthew 6:5-15). He said, in effect, "don't pray like the Pharisees who love to be heard in public for the impression that they can make. Rather pray in private. Go into your own room and close the door and pray there". Jesus also gave his disciples "The Lord's Prayer"--teaching the disciples, and through them teaching us, a sound model for prayer.

Toward the end of his ministry, as Jesus was speaking of the end of the age and of his return, he said, "Pray that your flight is not in winter" (Matthew 24:20). He said to the disciples, "Watch and pray that you do not enter into temptation" (Luke 22:46). Jesus said that we are to pray for those who abuse us (Luke 6:28). We are to pray for those who are unkind to us. It is a great blessing to learn to pray for people who are our enemies and for people whom we do not like. God does a work in our lives as a result of our praying. Jesus told the parable of the unrighteous judge and the persistent widow, who had her case settled by the judge because of her importunity even though he thought it was a trivial manner unworthy of his attention. She hung in there until he settled her case. Luke says that Jesus told this parable, to the effect, "that they ought always to pray and not lose heart".

Meaningful prayer requires effort on the believer's part. Human inclinations to laziness are enemies of an effective prayer life. We are so accustomed to things being made easy for us that we quickly become disinclined toward worthwhile activities that require effort. A. W. Tozer points out that people are frequently impatient with the processes of sanctification:

> By trying to pack all of salvation into one experience, or two, the advocates of instant Christianity flaunt the law of development which runs through all nature. They ignore the sanctifying effects of suffering, cross carrying and practical obedience. They pass by the need for spiritual

training, the necessity of forming right religious habits and the need to wrestle against the world, the devil and the flesh.

In Luke 10:2 we read of Jesus' instruction to his disciples to pray: "Pray the Lord of the harvest to send out laborers into his harvest.". The apostle Paul, writing to the church of Colossae gave a similar exhortation:

> Continue steadfastly in prayer, being watchful in it with thanksgiving; and pray for us also, that God may open to us a door for the word, to declare the mystery of Christ ...
> [Colossians 4:2,3]

Jesus set an example for us in prayer. We read in Luke 6:12 (prior to his appointment of the twelve apostles from a larger group of disciples), "in these days he went out into the hills to pray: and all night he continued in prayer to God." John, chapter 17, gives us Jesus' "Great Prayer"--as he prayed regarding his relationship with the Father--as he prayed for the disciples--as he prayed for those who were yet to believe in him. We also read in the gospels of Jesus praying in the Garden of Gethsemane immediately prior to his arrest, trials, and crucifixion. In his life of prayer Jesus sets an example for us. If it was important for the mighty Son of God to pray--it surely is important that prayer be a substantial part of every believer's life.

As we read of the beginnings of the church in the book of Acts--we see that prayer was not peripheral--it was at the very heart of the believing community. The ministries of these early Christians flowed out of prayer. On at least thirty different occasions, in the book of Acts, prayer is seen as central to the work of the church. One hundred and twenty believers in Jerusalem prayed together after the ascension of Jesus before they chose a new apostle to replace Judas. At that time they prayed daily for ten days, and then the great outpouring of the Holy Spirit came at Pentecost. We read in Acts, chapter six, that one of the reasons given for the selection of the first seven deacons was to enable the apostles to continue to give priority to prayer.

Prayer is one of those vital matters that can be pushed aside by other things that seem more pressing--more of the moment--more urgent. All too frequently the urgent crowds out the important. The first seven deacons were selected to ease the administrative responsibilities of the apostles because they were determined that prayer would continue to be central in their ministry. When one of those deacons, Stephen, was executed by wicked mob violence—his last recorded words are of his prayer for those who executed him. When Saul of Tarsus met Christ on the road to Damascus and was taken into that city--he prayer fervently. Peter was praying on a rooftop in Joppa when the messengers came from Caesarea to take him to the household of Cornelius. Surely that time of prayer helped to prepare Peter to share the gospel with Cornelius and those associated with him.

The importance of prayer is again underlined as we read of the ministry of the church in Antioch. Before Paul and Barnabas began the first missionary journey the members of that church were engaged in a period of fasting and praying. The great missionary endeavors of Paul and his associates were initiated and undergirded with the prayer of the church in Antioch. On the second missionary journey Paul and Silas and others were ministering in Philippi. Paul and Silas were falsely accused before the magistrates and unjustly jailed. While in jail they prayed and sang hymns. A most unusual response to such an act of injustice! Their prayer and devotion to God caught the notice of other prisoners and of the jailer himself. He and his household believed in Christ, and were baptized that very night. The Eerdman's Analytical Concordance to the Revised Standard Version of the Bible lists approximately four hundred and fifty references to prayer in the Old and New Testaments. Prayer is a subject of primary importance.

Prayer is not magic. Recall the story of Aladdin's lamp. All that Aladdin had to do was to rub the lamp three times and the genie appeared, and the genie did anything that Aladdin asked him to do. We recognize that as a pagan concept of prayer. The idea of magic is that by the right incantations or procedures one can control the supernatural. If one observes the correct formula-- the supernatural is at one's beck and call. That pagan concept creeps into the Christian doctrine of prayer. We must be on guard against elements of superstition in our practice of prayer (or teaching regarding prayer). We cannot separate God from his power! God and his power are one and the same. We cannot draw on God's power, contrary to his will and purpose, by the right praying methodology.

The person who prays must be in harmony with God. This does not mean that we have to live perfect lives. If that were so there-would never be any answered prayers for human beings. Nonetheless, in order to engage in effective prayer we have to be in tune with God's purposes and goals.

> "If you abide in me, and my words abide in you, ask whatever you will and it shall be done for you." [John 15:7]

PREREQUISITES FOR PRAYER

1. *Belief in Christ.* I do not mean to imply that the only prayers God answers are Christian prayers. There are some indications in scripture that God, in his sovereign will, may choose to respond to the prayer of the pious unbeliever. In any event, we want to respect God's sovereignty. We are not going to take the position of telling him what he can and cannot do. But our confidence in prayer is in and with Jesus Christ who is our Savior, who is seated at the right hand of the Father interceding for those who trust in him.

> Since then we have a great high priest who has passed through the heavens, Jesus, the Son of God, let us hold fast our confession....Let us then with confidence draw near to the throne of grace, that we may receive mercy and find grace to help in time of need. [Hebrews 4:14 and 16]

2. *Faith.* God expects people to come with confidence to him in prayer. Faith and doubt in regards to prayer are at opposite ends of a continuum. Few approach God with absolute faith, but it is important to be moving in the direction of faith and away from doubt.

> And whatever you ask in prayer, you will receive, if you have faith. [Matthew 21:22]

> I say to you, if you have faith as a grain of mustard seed1

you will say to this mountain, 'Move from here to there,' and it will move; and nothing will be impossible to you.
[Matthew 17:20]

But let him ask in faith, with no doubting, for he who doubts is like a wave of the sea that is driven and tossed by the wind. For that person must not suppose that a double-minded man, unstable in all his ways, will receive anything from the Lord. [James 1:6-8]

Following the tremendous exultation of the transfiguration experience, Jesus with Peter, James, and John came down the mountain and found the other disciples unable to heal an epileptic boy. Jesus rebuked his disciples for their little faith in this matter. He told the father of the boy that the healing of his son was possible if he would believe. We then read,

Immediately the father of the child cried out and said, "I believe; help my unbelief!" [Mark 9:23]

God knows our struggle for faith. But it is clearly his will that we move toward faith--not away from it. Faith is not self-confidence so much as it is God-confidence: that he is good; that it is his desire that we pray; that he is well able to perform what we ask of him.

3. *Obedience.* No one who believes in Jesus Christ is free from sin. Having said that, commitment to Jesus Christ can make a remarkable difference in a person's life. We are enjoined to do what our Savior bids us to do. Since the best Christian only imperfectly serves his master, what is the difference? It must be that some have a genuine desire to do the will of God, however imperfectly or incompletely, while others seek to subvert the will of God. An obedient spirit is closely associated with effective prayer.

Behold, the Lord's hand is not shortened, that it cannot save, or his ear dull, that it cannot hear; but your iniquities have made a separation between you and your God, and your sins have hid his face from you so that he does not hear. [Isaiah 59:1,2]

> When you spread forth your hands, I will hide my eyes from you; even though you make many prayers, I will not listen; your hands are full of blood. [Isaiah 1:15]

Why should we expect that God will move in our favor, if it is not his will that we ultimately desire?

4. *Forgiveness*. Jesus plainly taught that if we are to be assured that God will forgive our sins we must forgive others. Forgiveness is basic to one's relationship with God. Indeed, without forgiveness there can be no relationship. As we approach God, his forgiveness of our sins in Jesus Christ is vital. Therefore, for a person to retain an unforgiving spirit--is to demean God's forgiveness. It is to devalue God's forgiveness--to say that it is of little worth. In addition, if we believe that it is good for God to forgive us then we must also believe that it is good for us to forgive others.

> And forgive us our debts, As we also have forgiven our debtors; [Matthew 6:12]

> Then Peter came up and said to him, "Lord, how often shall my brother sin against me, and I forgive him? As many as seven times? Jesus said to him, "I do not say to you seven times, but seventy times seven. [Matthew 18:21,22]

Jesus told the parable (Matthew 18:23-35) of the servant who was forgiven an immense sum by his master and then sought to exact a small debt from one of his fellow servants, even having him put in prison. When the master heard of this servant's ingratitude--he ordered him placed in jail until he should pay the debt in full. It is surely most significant that it is in The Lord's Prayer (the model prayer) that Jesus teaches us to affirm our willingness to forgive others the wrongs that they have done to us.

FURTHER EFFECTS OF PRAYER

Mark 13:18 is a most significant verse on prayer, "Pray that it may not happen in winter." This is the section of the gospel of Mark that corresponds to Matthew, chapter 24, and Luke, chapter

21, regarding the end of the age. I believe that Jesus has two convulsive events in view: the destruction of Jerusalem by the Romans in 70 A.D. and some terribly cataclysmic events prior to the return of Christ. Jesus teaches that people are to pray that these events not come in winter when their severity would be intensified. In other words, even regarding the final events of our age, prayer can make a difference! There is a tendency to approach prayer fatalistically. Since God is sovereign, infinite, all knowing, all powerful, and his will is absolutely perfect--it is very easy to reason that our prayers cannot alter the course of events. One might well draw such a conclusion, except that the Bible does not allow us to. Again and again we are told that our prayers make a difference. We are surely incapable of explaining how time can make an impact on eternity--how man with the multitude of his limitations can make a difference with the God of the universe. But we are faced with the biblical affirmation that he can.

> Elijah was a man of like nature with ourselves and he prayed fervently that it might not rain, and for three years and six months it did not rain on the earth. [James 5:17]

> So Peter was kept in prison; but earnest prayer for him was made to God by the church. [Acts 12:5]

The parable of the importunate widow in Luke 18:1-8 clearly implies that it makes a significant difference when those who believe in God are persistent in prayer:

> And will not God vindicate his elect, who cry to him day-and night? Will he delay long over them? I tell you, hewill vindicate them speedily. [Luke 18:7,8]

The parable in Luke 11:5-13 of a man going to a friend of his at midnight and asking for three loaves of bread is unique to the gospel of Luke. It has a great deal to teach us about prayer. If you want to borrow something from your neighbor's kitchen you will probably go to him during the daytime or in the early evening, not at midnight! I am sure that Jesus had a sense of humor, and there is a humorous thread to this parable. The friend in need of bread is banging on the door trying to wake up someone in the house. Jesus tells us that the inclination, if not the actual response, of the friend that was being imposed upon would be to shout, "go away, we are all in bed, we don't want to be bothered". But the friend in need of bread keeps making a racket so that no one can sleep. At this point Jesus states,

> I tell you, though he will not get up and give him anything because he is his friend, yet because of his importunity he will rise and give him whatever he needs. [Luke 11:8]

Jesus is not teaching that God sleeps and must be awakened, nor that he is bothered by our prayers. The point is that God rewards those who come to him with expectancy. Faith and constancy and persistence are closely associated. God is willing to bless--but he is waiting on those who believe in him to faithfully call upon him—seeking those things that they need and desire. Jesus was emphatic regarding the significance of this parable, saying,

> Ask, and it will be given you; seek, and you will find; knock, and it will be opened to you. For every one who asks receives, and he who seeks finds, and to him who knocks it will be opened. [Luke 11:9,10]

Charles Haddon Spurgeon said,

> Asking is the rule of the kingdom. Ask and ye shall receive....if the royal and divine Son of God was not exempted from the rule of asking, you and I cannot expect the rule to be altered in our favor.

WHAT IS TO BE THE SUBSTANCE OR SUBJECT MATTER OF PRAYER?

The possible subject matter of prayer cannot be exhausted, but certainly the outlines of prayer are suggested in the Bible and some particular themes of prayer are emphasized and illustrated. The Lord's Prayer is surely a primary resource for the content of prayer. It includes at least five elements:

a. Adoration and worship of God

b. The realization of the kingdom and rule of God

c. Daily bread (material needs for livelihood--which are not to be taken for granted)

   d. Forgiveness of sins

   e. Deliverance from evil

    We have already noted how both Jesus and Paul give very specific instructions regarding matters to pray about. We should carefully study the content of the many prayers in the Bible to examine their emphasis and understand their major concerns. From them we get a general outline that is quite similar to that of the Lord's Prayer:

   a. Adoration, Praise, Worship

   b. Thanksgiving

   c. Petition for forgiveness and acceptance with confession of sin

   d. Intercession on behalf of others

   e. Benediction

    In order to more fully understand the teachings of the Bible on prayer we need to understand what the Bible is getting at. What are the great goals that God has for those who are instructed to pray?

    a. The worship, adoration, and enjoyment of God including reflection on his majesty, greatness, and grace

    b. Expression of personal belief and trust in God; acknowledgement of faith in Jesus Christ

    c. The growth of the believer in grace to the end that he becomes more and more like Jesus Christ

d. The proclamation of the gospel to the ends of the world

e. The culmination of the purposes of God resulting in the return of Christ and the full establishment of the kingdom of God

> Prayer is the simplest form of speech
>   that infant lips can try;
> Prayer, the sublimest strains that reach
>   The Majesty on high.
>
> Nor prayer is made by man alone;
>   The Holy Spirit pleads,
> And Jesus, on the eternal throne,
>   For sinners intercedes. [James Montgomery]

Further Reading

The Gospel of John 17:1-26
The International Standard Bible Encyclopaedia, article on Prayer
Lockyer, Herbert, *All The Doctrines of the Bible,* XXIX, The Doctrine of Prayer
Myers, Warren and Ruth, Pray, *How to be Effective in Prayer,* NavPress

For Reflection or Discussion

1. Can you give a simple definition of prayer?

2. What areas of prayer or kinds of prayer do we most need to develop in our lives?

3. What are some steps that you can take to become more effective in prayer?

CHAPTER ELEVEN

THE KINGDOM OF GOD

The term (or the concept) of the kingdom of God is mentioned approximately one hundred and fifty times in the New Testament. In fact, Jesus spoke so frequently of the kingdom of God that one might well say it was his major subject. The importance of this theme is underscored in that Jesus made it quite plain that those who believe in him participate in God's kingdom. Those who reject him, who do not believe in him, are not included in his kingdom. A growing understanding of the nature of that kingdom can be a most helpful guideline as one grows in his day to day relationship with Jesus Christ.

The idea of a good kingdom is deeply imbedded in human nature. Many fairy tales tell of a good prince and princess and of their benevolent rule. The governance described or implied in such stories is in sharp contrast to what real governments are like.

The prince will be generous, farsighted, altruistic, considerate-- always looking out for the welfare of his people--never putting his needs or desires (or those of his cronies) ahead of theirs. The story of Snow White ends with the prince taking Snow White away to spend the rest of her life with him. But the implication is that he will become king and she will reign as queen. Rather than the misuse of power, there will be a wonderfully good government!

Sometime ago I saw the film, "The Lion in Winter". It has to do with Henry II of England (c. 1100-1200 A.D.). My curiosity is always evoked when I see films that purport to be dealing with historical persons and events. Has what I have seen in the film any relationship to what we know from history? As a consequence I did some reading about Henry II. I discovered that the film does an excellent job of portraying one segment of Henry's life. It vividly dramatized his vices! But it neglected an adequate portrayal of his strengths. It gave little attention to his virtues. As a matter of fact, Henry II was a highly regarded monarch. He was widely popular because he brought strong government to England and France after a period of disorganization, egregious injustice, and anarchy. In spite of his considerable shortcomings, his people appreciated the strength of his government. People long for assured, honest, dependable, reliable government!

In the book of I Samuel we read of Samuel, one of the great prophets and judges of Israel. Samuel brought impressive stability to the clans of Israel. Prior to Samuel the background of the period of the judges is one of disorganization, lawlessness, and near anarchy. As a result, the clans of Israel were vulnerable to the Philistines on the west and a number of nomadic tribes on their south and east. The people of Israel longed for the strength and solidarity that they presumed a king would bring to them. They importuned Samuel to give them a king, and in due course Samuel anointed Saul as the first king of Israel. And the promise of God was given to Saul's successor, David, that one of his descendants would be the truly great king that people have always longed for.

Jesus was welcomed into Jerusalem by a great multitude on Palm Sunday. Many misunderstood the nature of Jesus' kingship. But they knew that they wanted a good king, and they welcomed Jesus as their king. The complete fulfilment of all legitimate human hopes and aspirations is found in Jesus Christ. He will establish the final and lasting government. Peace will be permanently established. There will be no more warfare; no crime; no injustice. He is the one who is fit to be the ruler of the universe.

> For to us a child is born, to us a son is given; and the government will be upon his shoulder, and his name will be called "Wonderful Counselor, Mighty God, Everlasting Father, Prince of Peace." Of the increase of his government and of peace there will be no end, upon the throne of David, and over his kingdom, to establish it, and to uphold it with justice and with righteousness from this time forth and for evermore. [Isaiah 9:6,7]

Jesus spoke frequently and fervently of the kingdom of God.

From the New Testament we perceive three aspects to the kingdom of God: <u>First</u>, it is a continuation of the Old Testament kingdom of Israel. There is a continuity--a connection between the Old Covenant and the New Covenant; between the kingdom of Israel and the kingdom of God. I know that there are those who make an absolute separation between the kingdom of Isreal and the kingdom of God. For some this comes out of a concern to preserve the continuing identity of Israel. In order to do that they play a game of biblical leap frog. That is, they acknowledge virtually no connection between the Old Testament kingdom of Israel and the New Testament kingdom of God. Rather the Old Testament kingdom is seen as leap frogging the New Testament and the ensuing 1900 years of Christian history and landing in 1948 A.D. with the foundation of the new nation of Israel. Others look at the modern state of Israel as an aberration, as a fluke, with no connection to the Bible. A study of the Old Testament should make it rather clear that there is a connection. But it is not necessary to use the leap frog technique to maintain that connection.

There is ample teaching in the Old Testament that there is to be a renewed nation of Israel and that the descendants of Abraham, Isaac, and Jacob, which have been scattered across the world, will return to that land that God gave to Abraham and his descendants. We are dealing with two branches of the same river. One stream moving on the surface has flowed out of the Old Testament through the New Testament down to the present. It can be identified with the church. The other stream has been subterranean. It has the same source as the one that has been visible through history. It has been less visible--although always identified with the Jews. The new nation of Israel is in all probability the precursor of the restored kingdom of Israel of which the prophets wrote.

There is, then, to be a renewed kingdom of Israel. Nonetheless the kingdom of God is the legitimate successor of that Old Covenant kingdom that began with Abraham, Isaac, and Jacob. Under Moses and his successors that coalition of clans became a national kingdom within a described territory and with a definite governmental identity. Its citizens could be identified by their ancestry--by means of their genealogy. They were to be exhibit "A" of what it means to believe in God and worship him. They were to so manifest the glory of God that they would be a light to the other nations of the world--that other peoples might be drawn to God and believe in him (Isaiah 49:6 and 60:3). Ultimately they failed in this assignment. They turned inward. That inward attitude is illustrated in Jonah's extreme reluctance to tell another

The Major Themes of the Bible

nation about the true God. They congratulated themselves on their special standing with God. They did not effectively show him forth to the other nations.

That Israel was a part of the kingdom of God is confirmed in the system of worship that God gave to them and in the constitution which he gave to them: the heart of which was the Ten Commandments. they were under the rule of God and, thus, they were a part of God's kingdom. The New Testament builds upon the Old. It does not start from scratch.

However, under the New Covenant, the kingdom of God transcends national boundaries and race or genealogy. The book of Acts describes the struggle that the early believing community went through in recognizing this transition. No longer is it a matter of where one lives or whom one's ancestors are. Rather, it is a matter of allegiance to Christ. The kingdom of God involves faith in Jesus Christ--walking with Jesus Christ--obeying Jesus Christ-- doing his work and his will. The continuity between the kingdom of Israel under the Old Covenant and the New Testament kingdom of God is illustrated in a number of Jesus' statements. Matthew 21:43 relates that Jesus said,

> Therefore I tell you, the kingdom of God will be taken away from you and given to a nation producing the fruits of it.

It is quite evident as we study other passages in the New Testament that the other nation Jesus refers to is the church. The church is the people of God who believe in Jesus Christ and who accept God's reign and rule over their lives. Matthew 8:11,12, tells us that Jesus said,

> I tell you, many will come from east and west and sit at table with Abraham, Isaac, and Jacob in the kingdom of heaven, while the sons of the kingdom will be thrown into the outer darkness; there men will weep and gnash their teeth.

It is apparent that some of those who are descendants of Abraham will be excluded from this kingdom. But others who believe in Jesus will be included. Under the New Covenant there is to be a new identifying factor: faith and obedience. Matthew 7:21,

Not every one who says to me, Lord, Lord, shall enter the kingdom of heaven, but he who does the will of my Father who is in heaven.

It is implicit in the relationship between a king and his people, that the people recognize his sovereignty, that they are obedient to him, that they do his will. There is a continuity between the kingdom of Israel and the kingdom of God. But there is a filling out of the kingdom of God in the teachings of Jesus that we do not find in the Old Testament.

Second, the kingdom of God has arrived. It is a present reality. To be sure its fulfillment awaits the future. But it is also present. Jesus announced the arrival of the kingdom coinciding with his earthly ministry. So did John the Baptist. That was more than nineteen hundred years ago. If it arrived with the ministry of Jesus, it surely must be here now. Luke 10:8,9,

> Whenever you enter a town and they receive you, eat what is set before you; heal the sick in it and say to them, "The kingdom of God has come near to you.'

> But if it is by the Spirit of God that I cast out demons, then the kingdom of God has come upon you.
> [Matthew 12:28]

Jesus announced the presence of the kingdom. One does not have to wait for it. As soon as one believes in Jesus Christ and begins to follow him, he is a citizen of the kingdom of God. The kingdom of God has more to do with inner commitment than with formal religion. It has much more to do with spiritual values than with material. The Old Covenant had to do with the law and an elaborate system of worship. The New Covenant has to do with faith in Christ and liberty. Because the Holy Spirit now takes up residence in the life of the believer, he has the opportunity of serving Jesus Christ out of love.

Third, the kingdom of God is to receive allegiance over anything else. Jesus said, "But seek first his kingdom and his righteousness, and all these things (that is, temporal needs) shall be yours as well." Jesus spoke with definiteness of the priority that was to be given to the kingdom by those who believe in him. Mark 9:47 is one of many passages that could be cited,

> And if your eye causes you to sin, pluck it out; it is better for you to enter the kingdom of God with one eye than with two eyes to be thrown into hell,

Jesus was speaking metaphorically, but the point is that nothing is to interfere with ones relationship with God. Again Jesus said,

> If any one comes to me and does not hate his own father and mother and wife and children and brothers and sisters, yes, and even his own life, he cannot be my disciple.
> [Luke 14:26]

One should not stumble over that passage with an unduly literalistic interpretation. Jesus is not teaching people to hate. That would be contrary to everything else that he taught. He is saying by way of analogy, that no human allegiance is superior to that between the believer and his Savior.

In one sense, we are enamored with the truth. We love information. We read the newspapers--we peruse the news magazines--we listen to the latest news. In our daily conversations we continuously seek more information. We want to find out if anything has happened that we did not know about. We are interested in new truth. But we are not always interested in commitment. There is a difference between enlightenment and commitment. There is a difference between knowing what one ought to do and doing it. Jesus illustrated that difference in the parable of the five wise and the five foolish virgins. The time for a wedding celebration was approaching. The marriage arrangements of that time were quite different from twentieth century engagements. The ceremony was not fixed weeks ahead for a specific time. There were no printed announcements giving the time and the place of the wedding and then of the reception to follow. In the culture of Jesus' day, ordinarily, the betrothal had been agreed upon by the parents of the bride and groom years before. The season for the wedding having arrived--all who are to participate are to be in readiness. But the bridegroom is possibly coming from some distance, with uncertainty as to the time required for travel, and, then, he must spend time with the bride's family and at last bring her with him to the wedding feast.

All ten of these young women knew that they must be ready for the arrival of the bridegroom, even though they did not know the precise time of his arrival. Five were prepared; they secured oil for their lamps. Five were unprepared and were excluded. The kingdom of God involves more than enlightenment and understanding. It involves the commitment of one's life to the Lord. Think of a great sailing vessel representing the kingdom of God. The believer gets on board and his commitment is so complete that he is determined to stay with it whatever the weather, whatever the seas, whatever the threat. Faith in Christ means that the believer does not have some alternate plan!

Participation in God's kingdom involves personal decision. There will only be naturalized citizens. If a person wants to be President of the United States he or she must be a native born citizen. If one comes from another country to the United States and becomes a naturalized citizen he will have every right and privilege of a native born citizen except one. He or she cannot become president. There is a distinction between the native born and the naturalized. The Bible teaches that there are no native born citizens in the kingdom of God. One enters it on ones own volition.

> But to all who received him, who believed in his name, he gave power to become children of God; who were born, not of blood nor of the will of the flesh nor of the will of man, but of God. [John 1:12,13]

Fourth, the fulfillment of the kingdom of God is in the future. The kingdom of God is a present reality. It is here now. But like the rosebud it awaits the full blossom. The believer should ask himself or herself; "Am I so enamored, so caught up, so involved with the affairs of this life that if Jesus returned it would be an inconvenience for me--an interference with my plans?" Or do you live your life with all of its responsibilities, nonetheless, looking forward to the return of Christ and the establishment of his kingdom? Christ will most certainly come--and the imperfect will be made perfect. The petition that we have been taught to offer in the Lord's Prayer, "Thy will be done on earth as it is in heaven", will be fulfilled.

The only stable, consistent, rational understanding of the significance of life comes from God. To the degree that a person departs from the biblical world-view, he loses his way and ultimately will become confused unable to distinguish right from wrong. Christ will return. His kingdom is coming. We are to pray for its full realization.

> Then the seventh angel blew his trumpet, and there were loud voices in heaven, saying, "The kingdom of the world has become the kingdom of our Lord and of his Christ, and he shall reign for ever and ever."

Even so, come quickly Lord Jesus!

Further Reading

Ladd, George Eldon, *Crucial Questions About The Kingdom of God*, Wm. B. Eerdmans Publishing Co.

For Reflection or Discussion

1. How is it possible for God's kingdom to be present, yet still coming in the future?

2. What is a key characteristic of the kingdom of God?

3. In what sense does Israel participate in the kingdom of God?

4. What can you do to make God's kingdom more of a present reality in your life?

CHAPTER TWELVE
THE AUTHORITY OF JESUS CHRIST

"Why do you call me, Lord, Lord, and not do what I tell you?"

The authority of Jesus Christ is one of the central themes of the Bible. It is affirmed in many places and in many ways:

If you love me, you will keep my commandments.
[John 14:15]

He who has my commandments and keeps them, he it is who loves me; [John 14:21]

Abide in me, and I in you. As the branch cannot bear fruit by itself, unless it abides in the vine, neither can you, unless you abide in me. I am the vine, you are the branches. He who abides in me, and I in him he it is that bears much fruit, for apart from me you can do nothing....If you keep my commandments, you will abide in my love, just as I have kept my Father's commandments and abide in his love. [John 15:4,5]

Let us briefly address the subject of authority in general. As one understands that a healthy structure of authority is important for every person--We will be more inclined to value and recognize the authority of Jesus Christ.

Authority has to do with the ordering of individual lives in such a way that people can work together in peace and safety-- and so that there is a consistent structure within which worthwhile tasks can be accomplished. Authority may be misused. Authority may be usurped. Authority may be exercised excessively. But without the proper exercise of reasonable authority, people are adrift--at sea--without a compass--without any sure point of reference. Authority provides the organizing principle so that the people and institutions that make up society can live and work together in safety and in harmony. Without properly constituted authority we are like those described in Ephesians 4:14, "children, tossed to and fro, and carried about with every wind..."

We end up believing one thing one week and another thing another week--following one concept or leader one time and quickly shifting as the sands shift according the the changes of the wind.

A bumper sticker, seen more frequently in the seventies and only occasionally now, reads, "Question all authority." If the thrust of that bumper sticker is that people should be on guard against abuses of authority, then it is well taken. On the other hand, it is quite naive if it infers that all authority is to be despised. There is absolutely no way that authority can be abolished from human society. All that can be done is to shift its locus; change its position. Authority may reside in a despot or, in a situation of near anarchy, it may be fragmented and transferred to the individual members of society or to micro-groups within that society. Either way there is a limit as to how far the locus of authority can be shifted, and it cannot be extinguished.

The situation in Lebanon in the late 1970s and during the 1980s is a case in point. It isn't that authority is absent in Lebanon. It is rather that the authority there has been tragically diffused. Authority has been usurped by so many different entities that law and order have ceased to exist. People who are forced to live with anarchy will ultimately find it so intolerable that they will come to prefer arbitrary despotism to the dangers and disorder of anarchy. It was a relatively short time from the anarchy of the latter days of the judges of Israel to the despotism of king Saul.

> In those days there was no king in Israel; every man did what was right in his own eyes. [Judges 21:25]
>
> Then all the elders of Israel gathered together and came to Samuel at Ramah, and said to him, "Behold, you are old and your sons do not walk in your ways; now appoint for us a king to govern us like all the nations."
> [I Samuel 8:5]

In contrast to the negative example of Lebanon is Dennis Conner, the skipper of "Stars and Stripes", the twelve meter yacht that was victorious over boats from many other nations and returned the coveted America's Cup from Australia to the United States in 1987. There were eleven men on those twelve meter boats: the captain, a bow man, the sewer man (the fellow who is down below during the race doing the dirty work of stowing sails and lines and supplying new sets), grinders, tailers, and a navigator. There were eleven men--but no one had any doubt where the authority resided on "Stars and Stripes". Dennis Conner was at the helm and in command! We know that without a very well defined authority, in a situation like that, not only would the boat not be victorious--it would not even sail well.

Those who established the Constitution of the United States of America recognized the need for strong central government, but they also recognized that governmental authority can be exercised abusively. Therefore, they provided for a separation of powers within the federal government and for a division of powers between that government and the individual states. The first ten amendments to the Constitution provided for protection of basic liberties from the power of government. Their solution to historic problems of the abuse of authority was not to exorcise authority but to define it as carefully as possible so that it might be useful rather than harmful.

I watched a debate between two guests on William Buckley's, "Firing Line", on the subject of sex education in the schools. An attorney representing Planned Parenthood affirmed the importance and usefulness of sex education in the schools, and a professor from Fordham University denied its value. The attorney put forth a point of view that we hear with disturbing frequency, but that is untenable. She endorsed values, but refused to countenance moral standards. When questioned on her position she adamantly refused to affirm any necessity for moral standards. She said that she would not use the term, morality. Although she refused to use that term, it was quite apparent that she held firmly to certain "values"--and that, in effect, these values functioned as moral standards for her even though she refused to recognize that fact. For example, one of her values was that young teenage girls, fourteen, fifteen, and sixteen years old should not become pregnant. But she refused to affirm any moral standards regarding the wrongness or rightness of promiscuous sexual intercourse among teenagers. I wished that someone would have asked her how she would feel if her purse were stolen. Could she only affirm a value that she prefers having her purse rather than not having it? Or that she prefers people who don't snatch purses over those who do? I wonder if she would not be driven to making a moral statement regarding thievery? Values alone will not work. Moral authority is a basic necessity.

Unless there is the undergirding of a firm moral order, life will not only be unhappy, it will eventually end in disaster. It is in that section in John's gospel where Jesus so clearly affirms his own authority that he says,

> These things I have spoken to you, that my joy may be in you, and that your joy may be full. [John 15:11]

There will be no joy when authority is misplaced or misused. And those who deny an objective, external source of morality have in the process appointed themselves the arbiters of morality! Many who decry the dreadful plague of AIDS are unwilling to admit that adherence to moral standards is important if the spread of that disease is to be arrested. They end up with an untenable position. They don't like for people to be sick. They don't like for people to die. But they are unwilling to effectively deal with the human behavior that leads to those terrible consequences.

If we are going to have moral values, sooner or later we must come to God. We must ask, where do moral standards arise and why do we have them? That is undoubtedly why some prefer to speak of values rather than morality. Because as soon as a person is willing to affirm that a specific action ought to be done or refrained from because it is right--then it is reasonable to ask, why is it right? Why ought it to be done or to be refrained from? Ultimately one can either appeal to God or he must acknowledge that morality is just a matter of personal preference--and one person's opinion is just as good as another's.

For the Christian, Jesus Christ is not only the Savior, Jesus Christ is the leader. Jesus is the master. Jesus is, indeed, our chief authority. If he is not, if there is some other authority greater than the authority of Christ, then we are idolators. Whenever we put some person or something in the place that belongs to Christ we have transferred our allegiance to another god. We no longer worship the true God. When we believe in Jesus Christ and recognize him as our Lord and master, we have entered the kingdom of God. The Bible presents dual truths regarding the kingdom of God: it is present in the lives of those who believe in Jesus Christ, and yet it is also future. We look forward to the completion, the fulfillment of the kingdom of God in association with the return of Jesus Christ.

Unfortunately, throughout history, including the present time, a great deal of energy has been wasted by Christians seeking to dilute or weasel out of the authority of Christ. The Christian should be alert to the continuing deceitfulness of sin. As the prophet, Jeremiah, said, "The heart is deceitful and desperately wicked, who can know it?" The Christian needs to be eternally alert lest avoiding the authority of Christ almost imperceptibly in small degrees--he ends up in a morass of disobedience that he would not have chosen had he seen the choice more clearly.

I. WHAT DOES THE BIBLE SAY ABOUT THE AUTHORITY OF JESUS CHRIST?

1. <u>He will be a ruler upon the throne of David forever</u>. An eternal reign is absolutely unique. It is not unique to have a prime minister, a president, a governor, or a king. But terms of presidents and prime ministers come to an end. Some royal dynasties have lasted for centuries--but they eventually terminate, and are succeeded by new dynasties or even totally new governments. But the scriptures declare that one of the descendants of king David will reign forever.

> your house and your kingdom shall be made sure forever before me; your throne shall be established for ever.
> [II Samuel 7:16]

> Once for all I have sworn by my holiness; I will not lie to David. His line shall endure for ever, his throne as long as the sun before me. Like the moon it shall be established for ever; it shall stand firm while the skies endure.
> [Psalm 89:35-37]

Isaiah 9:6,7 is one of the most familiar of the messianic passages. It also emphasizes the permanent continuing reign of the Messiah:

> For to us a child is born, to us a son is given; and the government will be upon his shoulder, and his name will be called "Wonderful Counselor, Mighty God, Everlasting Father, Prince of Peace." Of the increase of his government and of peace there will be no end, upon the throne of David, and over his kingdom, to establish it, and to uphold it with justice and with righteousness from this time forth and for evermore.

Daniel had a vision of Christ in which he looked forward to the everlasting reign of the Messiah:

> and behold, with the clouds of heaven there came one like a son of man, and he came to the Ancient of Days and was presented before him. And to him was given dominion and glory and kingdom, that all people, nations, and languages should serve him; his dominion is an everlasting dominion, which shall not pass away, and his kingdom one that shall not be destroyed. [Daniel 7:13,14]

The rule of Jesus Christ, the Messiah, the legitimate successor of David is again affirmed in the last book of the Bible:

> From his mouth issues a sharp sword with which to smite the nations, and he will rule them with a rod of iron; he will tread the wine press of the fury of the wrath of God the Almighty. On his robe and on his thigh he has a name inscribed, King of kings and Lord of lords.
> [Revelation 19:15,16]

2. <u>God has bestowed extraordinary honor upon him</u>. The Heavenly Father has bestowed honor upon Jesus above any other being. When we consider all of the honor and all of the authority that is conferred upon him, we see that he is, in every sense, equal with God the Father. Jesus said, "All things have been delivered to me by my Father;" (Matthew 11:27) He affirmed that the very words that he spoke were the words of God.

> So Jesus said, "When you have lifted up the Son of man, then you will know that I am he, and that I do nothing on my own authority but speak thus as the Father taught me.
> [John 8:28]

The apostle Paul in speaking of the humility of Jesus Christ in his incarnation, also, in the same passage spoke of his exaltation:

> Therefore God has highly exalted him and bestowed on him the name which is above every name, that at the name of Jesus every knee should bow, in heaven and on earth and under the earth, and every tongue confess that Jesus Christ is Lord, to the glory of God the Father.
> [Philippians 2:9-11]

Peter said that he is "exalted at the right hand of God" (Acts 2:33). The writer to the Hebrews declared,

> But we see Jesus, who for a little while was made lower than the angels, crowned with glory and honor
> [Hebrews 2:9]

As the disciples dispersed from Jerusalem into Judea, Samaria, Syria, and then throughout the Mediterranean world--they proclaimed that Jesus was Lord; that he was exalted in heaven seated at the right hand of God.

3. <u>He is the head of the church</u>. It is not the Pope in Rome or the Archbishop of Canterbury or the Metropolitan of Istanbul or the Stated Clerk of the General Assembly, the bishops of the Methodist Church, or the superintendents in the Assembly of God--but Jesus Christ who is the head of the church. Sometimes those who have been entrusted with responsibility in the church temporarily forget who is the head of the church! Jesus said of himself, "All authority in heaven and on earth has been given to me." The scriptures consistently affirm his headship of the church:

> and he has put all things under his feet and has made him the head over all things for the church, which is his body, the fulness of him who fills all in all.   [Ephesians 1:22,23]

> For the husband is the head of the wife as Christ is the head of the church, his body, and is himself its Savior.
> [Ephesians 5:23]

> He is the head of the body, the church; he is the beginning, the first-born from the dead, that in everything he might be pre-eminent. [Colossians 1:18]

Jesus Christ gave to his church very specific instructions as to its ministry both by his specific words of commissioning and by the example of his ministry. The book of Acts further explicates the will of Christ for his church as we see the early believers living out what they understand Christ's will to be for them. The church receives its authenticity from Jesus Christ, because he is its head.

II. WHAT ARE THE SOURCES OF THE AUTHORITY OF JESUS CHRIST?

Having affirmed the authority of Christ, let us now consider the sources of that authority:

1. <u>He is the very Word of God</u>.

> In the beginning was the Word, and the Word was with God, and the Word was God....And the Word became flesh and dwelt among us, [John 1:1,14]

> In many and various ways God spoke of old to our fathers by the prophets; but in these last days he has spoken to us by a Son, [Hebrews 1:1,2]

> He is clad in a robe dipped in blood, and the name by which he is called is The Word of God. [Revelation 19:13]

Jesus is the Word of God. He spoke the word of God. He is the ultimate authority. When he speaks, God speaks.

> He was still speaking, when lo, a bright cloud overshadowed them, and a voice from the cloud said, "This is my beloved Son, with whom I am well pleased; listen to him. [Matthew 17:5]

2. <u>Through him God created the universe</u>.

> all things were made through him, and without him was

The Authority of Jesus Christ

> not anything made that was made. [John 1:3]
> whom he appointed the heir of all things, through whom also he created the world. He reflects the glory of God and bears the very stamp of his nature, upholding the universe by his word of power. [Hebrews 1:2,3]

> for in him all things were created, in heaven and on earth, visible and invisible, whether thrones or dominions or principalities or authorities--all things were created through him or for him. He is before all things, and in him all things hold together. [Colossians 1:16,17]

Jesus is rightly referred to as the creator. It is literally by his power and authority that the created order came into being and continues to exist.

3. He is equal with God.

> Have this mind among yourselves, which you have in Christ Jesus, who, though he was in the form of God, did not count equality with God a thing to be grasped,
> [Philippians 2:5,6]

There is hardly a doctrine more clearly enunciated in the Bible than that of the divine nature of Jesus Christ. Some of the Old Testament messianic passages clearly inferred the deity of the Messiah. Jesus repeatedly claimed to be God and to be one with the Father. The gospel of John, at the very outset, declares Jesus' oneness with God in his eternity--in his creative power--and in his essence. It is especially in that gospel that Jesus affirmed his deity. Indeed, it was because his opponents understood this claim so clearly that they accused him of blasphemy and planned to arrest and kill him.

One cannot read the New Testament--and then deny that it clearly affirms the full deity of Jesus Christ--without emasculating it. That the Jehovah's Witnesses and other cults attempt to deny the clear teaching of the New Testament on Jesus deity--deprives them of any credibility when they attempt to appeal to scripture. If Jesus is God--he is one with the Father--he exercises the power of creation--he literally controls the universe--he is the law giver-- he is the source of truth--he will one day judge the world in righteousness. He is the source of authority. He is the rightful sovereign. He is, indeed, King of Kings and Lord of Lords. Because there are so many passages that plainly affirm his deity, that he is one with God, that he is God--I have included many of them as an appendix to this book.

4. <u>He is the author of our salvation</u>. We are obliged to Jesus Christ three times over. First, because he is our Creator--he made us--he brought us into being. Second, because he loves us and seeks us and provides for our salvation. Third, because he has redeemed us. He gave his life for our sakes. He has saved us. We are not our own. We are bought with a price. As God, he is our rightful sovereign. As our Savior he deserves our full allegiance. He is legitimately our Lord and Master. We rightfully acknowledge his authority. Those who reject or deny his authority--illegitimately convey to themselves or others prerogatives that belong only to God.

The practical effect of the authority of Jesus Christ is illustrated in the book of Acts, chapter four: Peter and John and other of the apostles were in the temple area proclaiming the good news of Jesus Christ. They were arrested by the temple authorities, and were questioned by them. Then they were ordered, by those authorities, not to speak or teach at all in the name of Jesus. Peter and John responded,

> Whether it is right in the sight of God to listen to you rather than to God, you must judge; for we cannot but speak of what we have seen and heard.   [Acts 4:19]

Ordinarily we are to be obedient to duly constituted authority, but when that authority conflicts with the clear will of God, the superior authority of God must always prevail.

Martin Luther found himself caught between the plain teaching of the Bible, on the one hand, and the authority of the church of his day (and of secular authorities that supported the church) on the other. Luther recognized that his first allegiance was to God. To obey the church and disobey the Bible would be to reverse the proper order of things. Charles Colson was an attorney and an important member of the Nixon administration. By his own admission he was so devoted to President Nixon that he was even willing to do wrong for him. But Charles Colson was renewed in Jesus Christ, and the authority of Christ was given its proper place in his life. Today Charles Colson glorifies God through prison ministries, writing, and a number of other areas. Attempting to please Jesus Christ is the central goal of his life.

Who is Lord? is the central issue. Who is the master of your life? About what or whom does your life revolve? Who is at the center of your universe? It is not a matter of what is convenient or what we are accustomed to or what others expect of us. In whom does sovereignty properly reside? If we recognize that, indeed, it properly derives from and is exercised by Jesus Christ, then how do we respond? What does he want you to do? Are you pleased with his purpose for you?

The hymn, "Crown Him With Many Crowns", appropriately expresses the rightful divine authority of Jesus Christ:

> Crown Him with many crowns, The Lamb upon His Throne;
> Hark! how the heavenly anthem drowns All music but its own;
> Awake my soul, and sing of him who died for thee,
> And hail Him as thy matchless King Through all eternity
>
> Crown Him the Lord of peace; Whose power a scepter sways
> From pole to pole, that wars may cease, Absorbed in prayer and praise;
> His reign shall know no end; And round His pierced feet
> Fair flowers of Paradise extend Their fragrance ever sweet.
>
> Crown Him the Lord of years, The Potentate of time;
> Creator of the rolling spheres, Ineffably sublime:
> All hail, Redeemer, hail! For Thou has died for me;
> Thy praise shall never, never fail Through-out eternity.

Further Reading

Romans 13:1-7
I Peter 2:13-17
Adler, Moritmer, *Ten Philosophical Mistakes*
Bloom, Allen, *The Closing of the American Mind*, Simon and

Schuster
Lewis, C.S., *The Abolition of Man*

For Reflection or Discussion

1. What are some possible sources of authority?

2. What are some important implications if we recognize that authority ultimately derives from God?

3. What alternatives are left to the person who refuses to recognize the authority of Jesus Christ?

CHAPTER THIRTEEN
THE CHURCH

> And I tell you, you are Peter, and on this rock I will build my church, and the powers of death shall not prevail against it. [Matthew 16:18]

> that through the church the manifold wisdom of God might now be made known to the principalities and powers in the heavenly places. [Ephesians 3:10]

> that he might present the church to himself in splendor, without spot or wrinkle or any such thing, that she might be holy and without blemish. [Ephesians 5:27]

Ekklesia, the word for church in the Greek New Testament, occurs approximately 110 times. The church is the gathering of those who believe in Jesus Christ, worship him regularly, pray together, are engaged in instruction together, eat together, enjoy fellowship together, are engaged in witness and ministry in the name of Jesus Christ, and welcome and baptize those who respond to their call to believe in Jesus. It is quite correct to say that outside of the church there is no salvation. Not that joining a company of Christians or going through whatever processes are required to become a member of a local church makes one a Christian. Christians are those who believe in Jesus Christ in their hearts and confess him with their lips. But the New Testament knows nothing of an isolated, individualistic Christianity. Those who believe in Christ are in the church! They become a meaningful part of a larger company.

> And they devoted themselves to the apostle's teaching and fellowship, to the breaking of bread and the prayers. [Acts 2:42]

The church is the body of Christ, and all who believe in him are members of it.

The word "church" in the English language is used in a dismaying number of ways. If is understandable if people become confused as to what exactly is intended by the word, church. The following are concepts that are conveyed by the use of the single word, church:

    a. the local congregation that comprises a particular church; i.e. First Methodist, Bethel Baptist, Emmaus Lutheran, etc.
    b. the property and buildings of the local church
    c. the Sunday worship service
    d. a denomination
    e. all churches and denominations taken together as a whole
    f. the entire Christian community from the time of Christ to the present

In this chapter I will use the word, church, most frequently for (e)--somewhat less frequently for (f), (d), and (a). I will not use the word at all for (b) and (c). Indeed, I think that (b) and (c) are unfortunate and misleading uses of the word. We should do our best to avoid using the word, church, as a designation of a physical facility or a piece of property or a particular worship service. For the church is the people--not the property. While the Sunday worship services are a vital function of the church, they are not in and of themselves the church. The church is the people of God!

The essentials of the church are as follows:

    a. an identifiable group of people who believe in Jesus Christ and have been baptized in his name

    b. regularly scheduled services of worship

    c. the proper administration of the sacraments of baptism and the Lord's Supper

    d. the people of God gathered for instruction, training, fellowship, and prayer

    e. service and witness engaged in and offered in the name of Christ.

The New Testament church is the proper successor to the Old Testament Israel. This is not to say that a continued Israel is thereby obliterated (I have dealt with the subject of the continuing identity of Israel in other chapters in this book). However, for the Christian community, the church took the place of the synagogue and, indeed, adopted the basic worship structure of the synagogue. The church belongs to Jesus Christ because it was founded by him. It is his body, he purchased it with his blood, and it is his bride which will be joined to him for all eternity. It began in intimate association with him, and is intended to continue with that intimate association through time and for all eternity.

The first Christian Pentecost (Acts, chapter two) may rightly be called "the birthday of the church". Thus, it may be convenient to trace the church back historically to the Pentecost events of Acts, chapter two. However, that birth was made possible by the foundational work that Jesus did in calling, training, and commissioning his disciples and in giving his life on the cross for all who would believe in him. Jesus Christ cares for his church because he loves it; because he left his earthly work in its custody; and because he has willed that its destiny be closely associated with his. That concern is evident not only in his earthly ministry and the final commissionings of his disciples--but, also, in Revelation, chapters two and three, where the risen Christ sends vital messages to seven churches in the Roman province of Asia.

From the beginning, the church has been threatened by false doctrine. Jesus warned against the enemy who would sow tares among the wheat. Paul warned the Ephesian elders of wolves that would invade their midst (Acts 20:29). The New Testament letters are replete with warnings against false teachers and false prophets:

> Beware of false prophets, who come to you in sheep's clothing but inwardly are ravenous wolves.
> [Matthew 7:15]

> But false prophets also arose among the people, just as there will be false teachers among you, who will secretly bring in destructive heresies, even denying the Master who bought them, bringing upon themselves swift destruction.   [II Peter 2:1]

> For such men are false apostles, deceitful workmen, disguising themselves as apostles of Christ.
> [II Corinthians 11:13]

The basic model for the church is set in the New Testament and especially in the book of Acts and in certain of the letters. The governance function of the office of apostle appears to have disappeared with the first century. However, the basic structure of pastors and elders and deacons has remained. The basic synagogue pattern of prayer, hymns, reading of scripture, and exposition of scripture, adopted by the early church, continues to be the worship structure of most Christian churches. To be sure that structure has been embellished quite a bit, especially in those churches that have made the mass the principle center of worship.

Originally elder and bishop were different names for the same office (see Titus 1:5-7 and Acts 20:17,28). No later than the second century the two names came to designate two distinct offices so that bishops would oversee several churches and eventually a considerable area. Then the further step was taken to archbishops (or metropolitans) and in the western church the papacy evolved. Thus, almost the entire Christian church had developed a highly structured hierarchical system until the beginning of the Protestant Reformation in the sixteenth century.

The power and authority of "the church" was not always used constructively. The crusades of the eleventh, twelfth, and thirteenth centuries were initiated and abetted by the church. They were an egregious misuse of the authority of the church and they contravened the clear teachings of Jesus and the New Testament.

> Then Jesus said to him, "Put your sword back into its place; for all who take the sword will perish by the sword.
> [Matthew 26:52]

> Jesus answered, "My kingship is not of this world; if my kingship were of this world, my servants would fight, that I might not be handed over to the Jews; but my kingship is not from the world." [John 18:36]

> For though we live in the world we are not carrying on a

worldly war, for the weapons of our warfare are not worldly but have divine power to destroy strongholds.
[II Corinthians 10:3,4]

The careful enumeration of the armor of God in Ephesians 6:10-20 should always put the church on notice that its instruments are not of the flesh.

Clearly, between the times of Jesus first and second advent, Jesus has committed his work on earth to the church. The church is the only organization founded by Jesus; it is the only one that he promised to work through and bless. The seven letters to the seven churches in Revelation, chapters two and three make it plain that Jesus Christ cares for his church, oversees his church, directs his church, purifies his church. If necessary he will remove a church (symbolized by a lampstand or candlestick).

Remember then from what you have fallen, repent and do the works you did at first. If not, I will come to you and remove your lampstand from its place, unless you repent.
[Revelation 2:5]

But his purpose is to maintain an effective church which obeys him and honors God.

Growth has been a characteristic of the church from the beginning. The addition of believers to the church is noted again and again by Luke in the book of Acts. This membership growth is seen in fulfillment of Jesus statement in Acts 1:8, and as an evidence of the continuing presence of the Holy Spirit with the church.

So those who received his word were baptized, and there were added that day about three thousand souls.
[Acts 2:41]

But many of those who heard the word believed; and the number of the men came to about five thousand. [Acts 4:4]

So the church throughout all Judea and Galilee and Samaria had peace and was built up; and walking in the

> fear of the Lord and in the comfort of the Holy Spirit it was multiplied. [Acts 9:31]

In his monumental work, *The History of the Expansion of Christianity*, Kenneth Scott Latourette documents the continuing growth of the Christian Church from the first century to the twentieth. There may have been a hiatus in the latter third of the first millennium A.D. as Islam expanded and the church became more and more insular. But, overall, membership growth has been a consistent and notable characteristic of the Christian Church.

Christ gave certain very specific tasks to his church. At the top of the list is the imperative to proclaim the gospel of Jesus Christ to the end that people believe in him. Proclamation, nurturing, training, and then sending forth are to be at the heart of the church's ministry.

> But you shall receive power when the Holy Spirit has come upon you; and you shall be my witnesses in Jerusalem and in all Judea and Samaria and to the end of the earth. [Acts 1:8]

The word of Christ is to be conveyed in such a way that those who believe are to be equipped to be teachers. In the "Great Commission" of Matthew 28:18-20, Jesus spoke not of making believers--but of making disciples, followers who would be adequately equipped to carry on his ministry.

I do not intend to claim that the church is restricted to the specific instructions given to it by Jesus or those found elsewhere in the New Testament. But the instructions of Jesus should certainly receive priority. The ministries of all churches should be congruent with and in proportion to the emphases found in the New Testament. Jesus taught specific identifying marks for his church:

1. Love (John 13:34,35)

2. Unity (John 17:11,20-23)

3. Obedience (John 14:21)

4. Witness (Matthew 28:19,20)

5. Hope/Patience/Faith/Confidence

The ultimate destiny of the church is to be ready for the return of Jesus Christ and to be united with him.

> ...Christ loved the church and gave himself up for her, that he might sanctify her, having cleansed her by the washing of water with the word, that he might present the church to himself in splendor, without spot or wrinkle or any such thing, that she might be holy and without blemish.
> [Ephesians 5:25-27]

> Then I heard what seemed to be the voice of a great multitude, like the sound of many waters and like the sound of mighty thunderpeals, crying, "Hallelujah! For the Lord our God the Almighty reigns. Let us rejoice and exult and give him the glory, for the marriage of the Lamb has come, and his Bride has made herself ready; it was granted her to be clothed with fine linen, bright and pure"--for the fine linen is the righteous deeds of the saints.
> [Revelation 19:6-8]

Further Reading

Latourette, Kenneth Scott, *A History of the Expansion of Christianity*, 7 vols., Zondervan

Little, Paul E., *Know What You Believe*, Chapter 7, "The Church, Victor Books

Schaff, Philip, *History of the Christian Church*, Eerdmans

Shannon, Foster H., *The Growth Crisis in the American Church*, William Carey Library

Thompson, Ernest Trice, *Through The Ages*, The Covenant Life Curriculum Press

Winter, Ralph, *The Twenty-five Unbelievable Years*, William Carey Library

For Reflection or Discussion

1 What is the main business of the church?

2. What are some essentials for a church?

3. What are some additional important ministries or activities of a church?

4. What is it that gives to the church its greatest importance?

CHAPTER FOURTEEN

THE BLESSINGS OF THE NEW COVENANT

> Neither is new wine put into old wineskins; if it is the skins burst, and the wine is spilled, and the skins are destroyed; but new wine is put into fresh wineskins, and so both are preserved. [Matthew 9:17]

> Therefore he is the mediator of a new covenant, so that those who are called may receive the promised eternal inheritance, since a death has occurred which redeems them from the transgressions under the first covenant.
> [Hebrews 9:15]

The word, "covenant", is a good biblical word. It is used well over one hundred times in the Old Testament, and it is used almost two score times in the New Testament. A covenant is a God-initiated agreement. In general usage a covenant is similar to a contract. But when God is involved, it is also quite different from ordinary contracts. Most of the agreements that people enter into to buy or sell or to perform some beneficial function for another person are mutual agreements. In legal parlance a "consideration" is involved; there is a quid pro quo--both parties give something and both parties receive something.

When it comes to one's basic relationship with God and God's covenant relationship with those who believe in him, the initiative is wholly on God's part. God drafts the contract! It is not for us to bargain over or change. He establishes the terms without consulting with us. We can only receive it and participate in it. Properly understood, response on our part to God's covenant is not optional.

You may go into an automobile showroom and look at the new cars. The salesman gives you a good sales talk and makes an offer to you on a car in which you have shown interest. You can decide whether or not to take the offer. You may like it or you may not like it. You may say either yes or no or you may bargain for a change in the offer. Someone may well contend that we can do the same thing with God. One can say yes to God or he can say no. And it is apparently true that a person can say no to God. But, in a sense, when God comes to us, presenting himself, his love, the sacrifice of his Son on the cross--there is really no alternative. There is no other offer on the table. It is the ultimate in foolishness to ignore or reject God's offer.

The biblical covenant is best understood in terms of God's call to certain people. God called Abraham (Genesis 12:1-3). One could say that Abraham did not have to respond to that call. He did not have to leave Haran in Mesopotamia. He could have remained associated with his father's household and the extended family there. But God's call was that he should respond, and Abraham responded. Recall in the first few chapters of the book of Exodus the account of God's call to Moses. Moses tried not to respond. He attempted to talk God out of the assignment. He told God that he surely must have a better person that him for the job. But the call of God came to Moses, and Moses obeyed. He was not successful in negotiating with God!

The call of God came to Jeremiah (Jeremiah 1:4-9), who protested the inappropriateness of that call because he was so young. Again God prevailed. Jeremiah entered into God's service on God's terms. Saul of Tarsus was confronted with a vision of the glorified, risen Jesus as he approached Damascus (Acts 9:3-6). Saul might have responded by acknowledging his mistakes and agreeing to quit his persecution of the Christian Church. He might, then, have proposed returning to Jerusalem and engaging in further study to clear his mind. But Jesus told Saul to go into Damascus--that he was going to be a witness for him. And that is what Paul did, and what he became. If one reads the account in Acts, chapter nine, of Paul's temporary blindness and his dependance upon others, it does not appear that Paul had any option other than to do what God told him to do! Years later, he said in his defense before King Agrippa,

> Wherefore, O king Agrippa I was not disobedient to the heavenly vision, but declared first to those at Damascus, then at Jerusalem and throughout all the country of Judea, and also to the Gentiles, that they should repent and turn to God, and perform deeds worthy of their repentance.
> [Acts 26:19,20]

The Blessings of the New Covenant

The call of God, which comes out of his covenant relationship, is an unequivocal call. It is extremely unwise not to respond.

I believe that we find five distinct covenants in the Bible:

1. <u>God's Covenant with Adam and Eve</u>. God created them in his image, placed them in a paradise, gave them to each other, and most wonderfully gave himself to them in fellowship. They broke their side of that covenant, and they experienced God's judgment: the unleashing of the terrible and inevitable consequences of sin.

2. <u>God's Covenant with Noah</u>. God promised Noah and his family deliverance from the impending judgment of the flood. He promised them (and through them all subsequent generations), that never again would he judge the world in the devastation of a universal flood. As a sign of his covenant with them, God placed his bow in the clouds.

3. <u>God's Covenant with Abraham</u>. God called Abraham to leave his family, friends, and homeland to go out to a place that God would show him. God brought Abraham and Sarah and Lot to the land of Caanan and promised to give that land to Abraham and to his descendants forever; to make of him a great nation; and to bless all of the people of the earth through him. God's covenant with Abraham is the foundational covenant of the Bible out of which the next two flow.

4. <u>God's Covenant with Moses and the people of Israel</u>. God delivered the people of Israel out of Egypt under the leadership of Moses, Aaron, and Miriam. On Mount Sinai he gave them the Ten Commandments, many other laws by which they were to be governed, and the rules and system by which they were to worship him. Again the covenant was God's. They could reject it, and some did. But they had no base to negotiate from. They could not amend it or change it. In effect, they tried to reduce the terms of the covenant by their wayward practices--but the judgment of God inexorably followed their faithlessness.

5. <u>The New Covenant that God establishes through his Son, Jesus Christ</u>. This covenant supersedes the others. It is related to

them. It is in fulfillment of them. But it does not abrogate them. For example, there are promises yet to be fulfilled under the Old Covenant to the physical descendants of Israel. This New Covenant is, however, far better and more wonderful than those which have preceded it.

These five covenants are, of course, not isolated and independent. They are interrelated. One logically follows another. This is especially true of the last three covenants. The covenant established by God through Moses on Mount Sinai was in fulfillment of God's covenant with Abraham. And the New Covenant, which comes in Jesus Christ, was implicit in those two covenants. However, it is sufficiently distinct to be designated a New Covenant. Thus, when we look at the Bible, from an overall perspective, two covenants stand out:

1. The Old Covenant that began with Abraham and that is further amplified and developed through Moses. The sacrificial system and the ceremonial law are closely associated with this covenant.

2. The New Covenant that comes through Jesus Christ

Let us consider the salient characteristics of the Old Covenant. Like all of the significant biblical covenants--it was initiated by God. God did not say to Moses, "Now I have some ideas regarding rules that you people probably should live by--if it doesn't inconvenience you too much. I want you to appoint a committee of the elders of Israel, and I want them to consider these rules to see if there are any alterations or additions that they would like to make. After they have considered the matter and responded--we will ratify the whole thing." NO! God gave them the Ten Commandments. He gave them his laws. He gave them their system of worship. God appointed a particular tribe to be the priestly tribe and a specific family within that tribe to be the priests. It was a God-given covenant.

That covenant was initiated in such a way that the holiness, the transcendence, the otherness of God was emphasized. In Exodus, chapter nineteen, one reads of a thick cloud--of lightening--of a mountain that trembled--of the shaking of the earth--and of a warning to the people that they must not even touch the borders of the mountain lest they die. That covenant emphasized the power and the holiness of God. It included God-given commandments, regulations, and laws for the nation.

The Old Covenant included God's provision for a specific system of worship utilizing the Tabernacle and its furnishings (later succeeded by Solomon's Temple). There was a large outer court and an elaborate tent covering the Holy Place and the Holy of Holies. The people of Israel were able to enter into the outer court, but they could not enter the Holy Place or the Holy of Holies. The priests could minister, as prescribed, in the Holy Place. Only the High Priest could enter the Holy of Holies, and he could do that only once a year on the Day of Atonement--and then only after carefully following specified preparations. This process emphasized forgiveness and healing and relationship with God. At the same time it impressed upon the people their distance from God--his holiness; their unworthiness.

God made certain wonderful promises to them. The grace of God is clearly demonstrated under that covenant. He promised to be their God and to give them a land flowing with milk and honey. He affirmed that they would be his people, that he would honor them above other nations, and that they were to make him known to the people of the world. In turn, they were to rightly worship him. They were to keep his laws. They were to observe the Sabbath. They were to eschew idolatry. They were to be a unique, peculiar people unto God--not intermingling with pagan peoples. God promised them great blessings, if they believed in him and obeyed him, and warned them of terrible consequences if they disobeyed. Unfortunately, all of the things that God told them not to do, they did. And most of the things that they were to do, they failed to do. They broke the covenant, and they experienced the fearful results of breaking that covenant.

That covenant was established with a particular people--a specific nation--the descendants of Abraham, Isaac, and Jacob. It is true that other people could be included. Provision was made for others to enter the household of Israel. And there are a number of indications that there were a significant number of others who believed in God outside of Israel. Nonetheless, that covenant was established with a specific people.

II Corinthians, chapter three, speaks of that Old Covenant and then about the New Covenant that is established through Jesus Christ. The book of Hebrews (especially chapters eight, nine, and ten) is particularly emphatic in delineating the benefits of the New Covenant. Like the Old Covenant, the New Covenant is also initiated by God. It is his provision--it is his love and his grace for all who will believe in him in Jesus Christ. But there are significant differences. Under the Old Covenant, God gave the laws and the system of worship to Moses. The people had no direct contact with God. Indeed, they were separated from him by a barrier with the warning that anyone who crossed over would die. Moses was unique in that era. The Bible tells us that God spoke to Moses person to person, as he had not done with any other human being.

> If there is a prophet among you, I the Lord make myself known to him in a vision, I speak with him in a dream. Not so with my servant Moses; he is entrusted with all my house. With him I speak mouth to mouth, clearly, and not in dark speech; and he beholds the form of the Lord.
> [Numbers 12:6-8]

In the New Covenant, God has now come near to his people. He has come from heaven to earth. He has taken human form being born as a baby of the Virgin Mary. He took upon himself flesh and blood so that the scriptures say of him that he was tempted in all points like we are yet, without sin. The book of Hebrews declares that it is especially appropriate for him to become our high priest because he has become like us. He understands our failings and our weaknesses first hand. God has come to us in Jesus Christ.

> Philip said to him, Lord, show us the Father, and we shall be satisfied. Jesus said to him, Have I been with you so long, and yet you do not know me, Philip? He who has seen me has seen the Father, how can you say, Show us the Father? Do you not believe that I am in the Father and the Father in me? The words that I say to you I do not speak on my own authority; but the Father who dwells in me does his works. Believe me that I am in the Father and the Father in me or else believe me for the sake of the works themselves.   [John 14:8-11]

Jesus said to the disciples, "No longer do I call you servants,...but I have called you friends,..." [John 15:15] How marvelous that the Creator God, the God of the universe makes himself known to all in Jesus Christ!

> who, though he was in the form of God, did not count equality with God a thing to be grasped, but emptied himself taking the form of a servant, being born in the likeness of men. [Philippians 2:5,6]

> For the law was given through Moses; grace and truth came through Jesus Christ. [I John 1:17]

This nearness of God, this coming of God to earth is also realized in the ministry of the Holy Spirit, which is discussed more fully in Chapter Nine.

> Nevertheless I tell you the truth: it is to your advantage that I go away, for if I do not go away, the Counselor will not come to you; but if I go, I will send him to you.
> [John 16:7]

Under the Old Covenant the person who was appointed High Priest would serve in that office for many years. But eventually the High Priest would die, and another High Priest would be appointed to succeed him. In addition to the High Priest there were many priests who represented the people in the daily offerings. The New Testament declares that Jesus Christ is now our High Priest. He did not offer the blood of bulls or goats, which had to be offered repeatedly. Those animal sacrifices were an anticipation--a symbol of the cross of Christ which was to come. As our High Priest, Jesus offered himself as the sacrifice presenting, his own blood before God the Father. Then he represents those who believe in him before the throne of God. He pleads their case. He is their advocate. God has come very close to us in the New Covenant through Jesus Christ. God has himself become our Savior.

This New Covenant is not limited to the descendants of Abraham, Isaac, and Jacob. It is for everyone. It is for both Jew and Gentile. It is for male and female. It is for rich and poor; sophisticated and simple; employer and employee. When that good news came into the first century Roman world it did not matter whether one was an Equestrian, a Patrician, Plebeian, Barbarian, Scythian, or slave. All who believe are brothers and sisters in Christ the Savior. The New Covenant transcends class, language, race, economic status, intelligence, and aptitude. Whoever will may come!

> There is neither slave nor free, there is neither male nor female; for you are all one in Christ Jesus.
> [Galatians 3:28]

> Therefore remember that at one time you Gentiles in the flesh, called the uncircumcision by what is called the circumcision, which is made in the flesh by hands--remember that you were at that time separated from Christ, alienated from the commonwealth of Israel, and strangers to the covenants of promise, having no hope and without God in the world. But now in Christ Jesus you who once were far off have been brought near in the blood of Christ. For he is our peace, who has made us both one, and has broken down the dividing wall of hostility, by abolishing in his flesh the law of commandments and ordinances, that he might create in himself one new man in place of the two, so making peace, and might reconcile us both to God in one body through the cross, thereby bringing the hostility to an end. [Ephesians 3:11-16]

As a person believes in Jesus Christ, he is united with all others who believe in him.

Under the New Covenant the Christian is set free from the bondage of the law. II Corinthians 3:6 reads,

> who has made us competent to be ministers of a new covenant, not in a written code but in the Spirit; for the written code kills, but the Spirit gives life.

This statement does not mean that when a person believes in Jesus Christ he can throw away the thirty-nine books of the Old Testament and pay only slight attention to the twenty-seven books of the New Testament. In a sense, under the Old Covenant those who believed in God were held to a rule book and measured by that rule book. There is greater freedom under the New

The Blessings of the New Covenant

Covenant, because the work of atonement is complete; it is no longer anticipatory--it has been fulfilled.

The believer relates to his Lord and Master, Jesus Christ, rather than to a written code. It is not that one is unaware of the Ten Commandments or that one can bypass them and other moral and ethical teachings in the Old Testament. It is that God, having come close to us in Jesus Christ, loving us in Jesus Christ--gives us the opportunity, indeed, the responsibility to love him in return. And in loving him we are to respond, not out of legalism, but out of a heartfelt desire to please him and to do his will. Thus, the apostle states, "For if what faded away came with splendor, what is permanent must have much more splendor." [II Corinthians 3:11]

The result of this is a new attitude toward the law--a shifting of gears, but not a disregard of the law.

> Now before faith came, we were confined under the law, kept under restraint until faith should be revealed.
> [Galatians 3:23]

> Therefore let no one pass judgment on you in questions of food and drink or with regard to a festival or a new moon or a sabbath. These are only a shadow of what is to come; but the substance belongs to Christ. [Colossians 2:16,17]

> Likewise, my brethren, you have died to the law through the body of Christ, so that you may belong to another, to him who has been raised from the dead in order that we may bear fruit for God. [Romans 7:4]

> So the law is holy, and the commandment is holy and just and good. [Romans 7:12]

> Now we know that the law is good, if anyone uses it lawfully. [I Timothy 1:8]

If the Old Covenant was a gracious blessing of God, the New Covenant is an even more gracious blessing.

> If that previous dispensation came with such splendor,

that the Israelites could not look at Moses' face because of it brightness, fading as it was, will not the dispensation of the spirit be attended with greater splendor?
[II Corinthians 3:7,8]

Those under the Old Covenant were blessed by God, but all who are under the New Covenant are even more richly and fully blessed. The writer to the Hebrews wonderfully summarizes that status under the New Covenant:

But you have come to Mount Zion and to the city of the living God, the heavenly Jerusalem, and to innumerable angels in festal gathering, and to the assembly of the first-born who are enrolled in heaven, and to a judge who is God of all, and to the spirits of just men made perfect, and to Jesus, the mediator of a new covenant, and to the sprinkled blood that speaks more graciously than the blood of Abel. [Hebrews 12:22-24]

A threefold response is appropriate to these marvelous truths: First Christians should be people of joy. I am sure you have seen people who win the jackpot on a big game show on television. They scream, jump up and down, hug everybody, and generally go wild. Their behavior is so predictable that one wonders if they have not been coached in how to respond should they win! Not a temporary hilarity--but an underlying quiet stream of joy should be characteristic of the one who believes in Jesus Christ. This does not mean that the believer is to be invulnerable to disappointment. Nor does it mean that he will be immune from the hurts and reversals of life. But Christians are spiritually rich. They have good news, and no one should be able to deprive them of the joy of their good fortune. The Christian should always know joy. We need, as the song says, to "count our many blessings, name them one by one". Humility, gratitude, thanksgiving, and joy are all closely interrelated.

Second, the believer's response should be one of worship and adoration. As we understand the nature of God (his holiness--his goodness--his immense power--the wonder of his love that he shouldcare for us), we should welcome regular opportunities for the public worship of God. The knowledge that, even though we have rebelled against him and have disobeyed him and gone contrary to his will, he has redeemed us and saved us in his Son,

The Blessings of the New Covenant

suffering his Son to die on the cross for our sakes--should cause one to make a substantial place in his life for devotion and worship. God is worthy that all should center their lives on him; that he should be more important than anything else to every person.

<u>Third, the believer's response should be one of commitment and involvement</u>. The book of James emphasizes that faith is dynamic--not static--not passive. Faith that exists in the heart should manifest itself in the way a person lives. A living tree produces leaves and fruit. In his very fine book, *Evangelism In The Early Church*, Michael Green discusses the dynamics of the Christian movement of the first three centuries. He seeks to understand why there was such dramatic and rapid growth in those early centuries. Why did so many people believe in Jesus Christ in spite of far greater obstacles than most Christians, outside of certain parts of the Communist and Islamic worlds, face today? Here is a brief statement from that book:

> The enthusiasm to evangelize which marked the early Christian is one of the most remarkable things in the history of religions. Here were men and women of every rank and station in life, of every country in the known world, so convinced that they had discovered the riddle of the universe, so sure of the one true God whom they had come to know, that nothing must stand in the way of their passing on this good news to others. As we have seen, they did it by preaching and personal conversation, by formal discourse and informal testimony, by arguing in the synagogue and by chattering in the laundry. They might be slighted, laughed at, disenfranchised, robbed of their possession, their homes, even their families, but this would not stop them. They might be reported to the authorities as dangerous atheists, and required to sacrifice to the imperial gods; but they refused to comply. In Christianity they had found something utterly new, authentic and satisfying. [Michael Green, *Evangelism In The Early Church*, Chapter Nine]

Believers should be people of joy--people who are rekindled in their devotion to God and who enthusiastically serve God out of gratitude for his goodness. The blessings of the New Covenant are real to them!

Further Reading

II Corinthians 3:4-18
Hebrews 8:1-9:28
Lockyer, Herbert, *All The Doctrines of the Bible,* Chapter IX, "The Doctrine of the Covenants", Zondervan

For Reflection or Discussion

1. Summarize the distinct benefits of the New Covenant

2. What can believers do so that they will reflect more of the joy that Jesus wants them to have?

3. What are some major impacts that the New Covenant should make on the lives of believers?

CHAPTER FIFTEEN

NEW LIFE AND SPIRITUAL GROWTH

Salvation is of God. It originates with him. It is his plan! The other side of God's initiative in salvation is the opportunity, indeed, the imperative for the individual to heed and respond. It is remarkably good news that God loves every person, and has made provision that everyone who will respond to him in faith will be saved. Recognizing this marvelous good news we may properly inquire, then what?

What is salvation? Is it fulfilled in being absolved of one's guilt and sin before God? Or is there much more to it than that? Please understand, I do not minimize the importance of that forgiveness and "salvation". Without the grace and forgiveness of God and the response of human faith and repentance--the sin of each human being becomes an insurmountable barrier between the individual and God. The ultimate purpose of forgiveness is the restoration of the relationship between God and the person whom he has created.

The person who believes in Jesus Christ has planted his feet in heaven. He or she has said, through belief and commitment to Christ, that their destiny is with God throughout all eternity. The scriptures make it quite plain that there are three phases in the believer's life: belief, growth, and glorification. Spiritual growth is to follow hard on the heels of belief. And glorification is the ultimate outcome as the believer enters the life to come. It is God's plan that those who believe in him grow in grace. Peter wrote,

> Like newborn babes, long for the pure spiritual milk, that by it you may grow up to salvation. [I Peter 2:2]

Ephesians 4:11-13, states,

> And his gifts were that some should be apostles, some prophets, some evangelists, some pastors and teachers, to equip the saints for the work of ministry, for building up

the body of Christ, until we all attain to the unity of the faith and of the knowledge of the Son of God, to mature manhood, to the measure of the stature of the fulness of Christ.

This passage from Ephesians makes it evident that belief and new birth is the beginning--not the end. The goal is to be like Christ--to be with Christ--to be spiritually mature.

Jesus spoke to Nicodemus about the need to be born anew. Birth implies growth! It is normal for the Christian to grow spiritually; abnormal for him not to do so. We are reminded of this by the apostle's remonstrance to the Corinthian Church:

> But I, brethren, could not address you as spiritual men, but as men of the flesh, as babes in Christ. I fed you with milk, not solid food; for you were not ready for it; and even yet you are not ready, for you are still of the flesh.
> [I Corinthians 3:1-3]

Spiritual growth is normal. The apostle expected it. He was keenly disappointed when he did not find evidence of it in many of the Corinthian believers. The entire theme of the book of Hebrews is that not only is it to be expected that the Christian will grow, but that it is dangerous not to grow. That every Christian should expect to be moving toward that maturity to which Christ has called him. This expectation of Christian growth is stated most plainly in Hebrews 5:12-14,

> For though by this time you ought to be teachers, you need some one to teach you again the first principles of God's word. You need milk, not solid food; for every one who lives on milk is unskilled in the word of righteousness, for he is a child. But solid food is for the mature, for those who have their faculties trained by practice to distinguish good from evil.

Sanctification is the theological word that is used for the process of Christian growth that is made possible by the Holy Spirit and is enabled by the believer's willing cooperation and participation. The most deliberate and complete statement of the principle of sanctification in found in Romans, chapters six, seven, and eight. However, the entire New Testament would become unintelligible if one did not recognize that spiritual growth is the norm--and that remaining static or backsliding are both abnormal and spiritually perilous. Thus, we read,

> Therefore, my beloved, as you have always obeyed, so now, not only as in my presence but much more in my absence, work out your own salvation with fear and trembling; for God is at work in you, both to will and to work for his good pleasure. [Philippians 2:12,13]

When the apostle Paul writes, "work out your own salvation with fear and trembling;" he has not abandoned the doctrine of salvation by grace alone, which he has so ably described. Rather he is recognizing that new birth and forgiveness--becoming children of God are at the beginning. God has a great deal more to do with the believer's willing cooperation. Perhaps no single passage expresses the purpose of God for those whom he redeems any more succinctly than II Corinthians 3:18,

> And we all, with unveiled face, beholding the glory of the Lord, are being changed into his likeness from one degree of glory to another; for this comes from the Lord who is the Spirit.

The grace of God is like an immense ocean. The scope of it overwhelms us. We cannot comprehend it. It is possible for a person to be so staggered by the grace of God that he lapses into spiritual irresponsibility and listlessness. This possibility is met head on in Romans, chapter six:

> What shall we say then? Are we to continue in sin that grace may abound? By no means! How can we who died to sin still live in it? Do you not know that all of us who have been baptized into Christ Jesus were baptized into his death? We were buried therefore with him by baptism into death, so that as Christ was raised from the dead by the glory of the Father, we too might walk in newness of life. [Romans 6:1-4]

That chapter in Romans goes on to remind us that willingly yielding one's self to sin leads to death, whereas yielding one's self to Christ leads to Christian growth and sanctification.

This reality of life in Christ is stated in II Corinthians 5:17,

> Therefore, if any one is in Christ, he is a new creation; the old has passed away, behold, the new has come.

This same truth is expressed in a somewhat different metaphor in the first Psalm,

> Blessed is the man who walks not in the counsel of the wicked, nor stands in the way of sinners, nor sits in the seat of scoffers; but his delight is in the law of the Lord, and on his law he meditates day and night. He is like a tree planted by streams of water, that yields its fruit in its season, and its leaf does not wither. In all that he does he prospers. [Psalm 1:1-3]

Some are sceptical of any true spiritual change in a person's life. Perhaps out of scepticism or out of keen disappointment John Stuart Mill wrote:

> To what an extent doctrines intrinsically fitted to make the deepest impression upon the mind may remain in it as dead beliefs, without being ever realized in the imagination, the feelings, or the understanding, is exemplified by the manner in which the majority of believers hold the doctrines of Christianity....These are considered sacred, and accepted as laws, by all professing Christians. Yet it is scarcely too much to say that not one Christian in a thousand guides or tests his individual conduct by reference to those laws....They are not insincere when they say that they believe these things. They do believe them, as people believe what they have always heard lauded and never discussed. But in the sense of that living belief which regulates conduct, they believe these doctrines just up to the point to which it is usual to act upon them...The doctrines have no hold on ordinary believers--are not a power in their minds. They have an habitual respect for the sound of them, but no feeling which spreads from the words to

the things signified,...Whenever conduct is concerned, they look round for Mr. A and B to direct them how far to go in obeying Christ.

John Stuart Mill is incisive in his description of some Christians, but certainly not of all Christians. To the degree that the above statements are true--they are a rebuke. Because it is right to expect that the believer will grow, and that in growing he will more and more exhibit the reality of Christ in his life.

Jesus taught that the greatest commandment is to love God. Imbedded within that commandment is the implication that we are to holistic in our love for God. Nothing in our lives is to be excluded from him. We are to recognize that everything that we have belongs to him and that everything of value derives from him. The word of God--his will--his purposes are to be of greater importance to us than anything else. Jesus illustrated this intimate relationship with God in John, chapter fifteen. He said,

> I am the vine, you are the branches. He who abides in me, and I in him, he it is that bears much fruit, for apart from me you can do nothing.   [John 15:5]

Jesus offended many who heard him when he said,

> Truly, truly, I say to you, unless you eat the flesh of the Son of man and drink his blood, you have no life in you; he who eats my flesh and drinks my blood has eternal life, and I will raise him up at the last day.   [John 6:53,54]

We recognize that Jesus frequently spoke in symbolic or metaphorical language. He said he was the vine. He said he was the door of the sheepfold. We should not take the above statement literally. But we must ask, what did Jesus mean?, What did he intend to convey? Was he not saying that the believer's relationship with him was to be one of closeness and intimacy? Our lives are to be wrapped up in him. In close association with him there are great possibilities of spiritual growth. Without him growth is impossible!

The apostle Paul wrote,

> I have been crucified with Christ; it is no longer I who live, but Christ who lives in me. [Galatians 2:20]

In John, chapter ten, Jesus referred to those who believe in him as his sheep. The metaphor is of a shepherd, with a relatively small flock, who knows and cares for each one of his sheep individually. To believe in God is to have a living, personal, daily relationship with him. He is to be the believer's friend; his closest associate. He is to mean more to the one who believes in him than anyone else or anything else in all of the world.

> Again, the kingdom of heaven is like a merchant in search of fine pearls, who, on finding one pearl of great value, went and sold all that he had and bought it.
> [Matthew 13:45,46]

Spiritual growth is the means whereby one comes into closer relationship with God. Many people have gardens or household plants. Plants can become very important to the person who cares for them. If one prepares the soil and plants the seed--and waters the plant--he will wait patiently for the growth to evidence itself. It is fully expected that the seed will sprout and grow and in due course blossom. When a tree is cut down, the age of the tree can be determined by counting its growth rings. As long as the tree lives, it will grow. Growth is natural; growth is normal. Jesus told the parable of the sower and the seed. It is obvious from that parable that God is looking for growth in the lives of those who believe in him.

It is God's desire that those who believe in him engage in ministry. Participation in ministry and service, in the name of the Lord, is an evidence of Christian growth. Jesus said to those who heard him, "Follow me, and I will make you fishers of men". (Matthew 4:11) We have noted his commissionings:

> All authority in heaven and on earth has been given to me.
> Go therefore and make disciples of all nations,
> [Matthew 28:18,19]

Ephesians 4:11-14 teaches that God gives the gifts of apostle, prophet, pastor, evangelist, etc. that the ordinary believer may be equipped for the work of ministry. Peter wrote,

> like living stones be yourselves built into a spiritual house, to be a holy priesthood, to offer spiritual sacrifices acceptable to God through Jesus Christ. [I Peter 2:5]

> But you are a chosen race, a royal priesthood, a holy nation, God's own people, that you may declare the wonderful deeds of him who called you out of darkness into his marvelous light. [I Peter 2:9]

The believer is not to be a spectator in the stands cheering the team on, he is to be down on the playing field actively engaged in the game.

In order to grow in the grace of God--to participate in the work of God--and to become increasingly effective in living for Christ and serving him--the believer needs vision and enthusiasm.

Isaiah wrote, "without vision the people perish". What is the source of this needed enthusiasm and vision? It comes out of the believer's life in Christ. The more real that relationship--the more likely the individual will be full of enthusiasm and vision for Christ's work. God especially identifies with us in Jesus Christ. We need especially to look at life through the eyes of Christ. As we study the gospels, we sense an evenness about the way Jesus approached life. He wasn't up one day and down the next. His perfect relationship with the Heavenly Father kept his vision for the Father's will and work clear. Our personal hope and the hope of the world is in God and his kingdom.

God provides the means whereby the believer is enabled to grow. We read of the 3000 who received Christ on that first Christian Pentecost,

> And they devoted themselves to the apostle's teaching and fellowship, to the breaking of bread and the prayers.
> [Acts 2:42]

Growth is normal, and a nurturing process is normal and expected in order to enable the believer to grow. Note the means of grace from Acts 2:42:

1. <u>The Apostle's Teaching</u>: Jesus and the apostles are not with us physically, but their words are recorded for us in Holy Scripture! The Bible is the word of God and it is the spiritual food for the believer. Daily Bible study is a cornerstone of Christian growth.

2. <u>Fellowship</u>: Christians are to be together in worship, in study, in social relationships, and in service to Christ. Jesus and the disciples and the early church are noted for their fellowship for their sticking together. They needed each other. In addition to Sunday worship, every Christian should be participating in some kind of small group with other Christians. These early believers were together for "breaking of bread" (Acts 2:42,46) Their relationship with one another was a means of strengthening their relationship with God.

3. <u>The Prayers</u>: Worshipping and praying together are normative; they are both essential and basic practices if spiritual growth is to take place. The writer to the Hebrews warned,

> not neglecting to meet together, as is the habit of some, but encouraging one another, and all the more as you see the day drawing near. [Hebrews 10:25]

The Psalmist stated,

> I was glad when they said to me, Let us go to the house of the Lord. [Psalm 122:1]

Jesus and the apostles worshipped regularly and prayed steadily. The believer should not presume that he can grow, and at the same time neglect the basic disciplines that the New Testament affirms to be essential.

If we desire wholeness of life--a strong sense of meaning in life--a world in which peace, justice, and goodness prevail--a world from which meanness and malice, prejudice, hatred, and violence have been banished--then God and his word and his purposes must be foremost for all peoples. The Heavenly Father has a great destiny for each person who believes in him.

> ...the Spirit himself bearing witness with our spirit that we are children of God, and if children, then heirs, heirs of God and fellow heirs with Christ, provided we suffer with him in order that we may also be glorified with him.
> [Romans 8:16,17]

> Therefore gird up your minds, be sober, set your hope fully upon the grace that is coming to you at the revelation of Jesus Christ. [I Peter 1:13]

> Therefore, brethren, be the more zealous to confirm your call and election, for if you do this you will never fall; so there will be richly provided for you an entrance into the eternal kingdom of our Lord and Savior Jesus Christ.
> [II Peter 1:10,11]

Further Reading

Lovelace, Richard F., *Dynamics of Spiritual Life* Chapter 6, "The Renewal of the Local Congregation"; Chapter 7, "The Sanctification Gap", Inter-Varsity Press

Shannon, Foster H., *God Is Light*, Chapter Fourteen, "A Balanced Spiritual Life; Chapter Fifteen, "The Christian Life is to be One of Growth"

Shelly, Bruce L., *Christian Theology in Plain Language,* Chapter 17, "The Family Likeness"

For Reflection or Discussion

1. What are the major barriers to spiritual growth for the Christian?

2. What are the best motivating factors for spiritual growth?

3. What passage of scripture appeals to you the most regarding Christian growth?

CHAPTER SIXTEEN

EVANGELISM AND WORLD MISSION

A Baptist minister had been speaking much too frequently on the subject of baptism, even in the opinion of his board of deacons. For six weeks running, baptism had been the major theme of every message and an overriding emphasis for as long as anyone could remember. So the deacons met with the pastor to discuss his excessive single-mindedness. They, of course, affirmed his good qualities and strengths in ministry. But they told him that the baptism theme was coming up too much, and that he needed to give attention to other subjects. They were delighted when he announced that on the very next Sunday his sermon would be on Adam and Eve. Sunday came and the Baptist preacher announced his text and the three main points of the message, First Point: "How Adam Got Into The Garden"; Second Point: "Why Adam Got Out of the Garden"; Third Point: "Water Baptism"!

In reverence and humility, I affirm that God is like that Baptist minister. It does not matter what the subject may appear to be, he always come back to his main theme. God's plan of redemption and salvation for the whole world is the consistent theme of scripture. Of all the themes this is THE theme. Early in the book of Genesis God called Abraham, but he was looking through Abraham at the whole world: "by you all the families of the earth shall bless themselves." [Genesis 12:3] Many passages in the Old Testament speak clearly of God's love and concern for all peoples.

> For I know their works and their thoughts, and I am coming to gather all nations and tongues and they shall come and see my glory, [Isaiah 66:18]

> At that time Jerusalem shall be called the throne of the Lord, and all nations shall gather to it, to the presence of the Lord in Jerusalem, and they shall no more stubbornly follow their own evil heart. [Jeremiah 3:17]

Thus, when Jesus commissioned the disciples to go into all the world he was not expounding a new concept. Rather he was giving specificity to what the Old Testament has already declared. When the council at Jerusalem wrestled with issues regarding the proclamation of the gospel to the Gentiles, James appealed to the Old Testament scriptures:

> Simeon has related how God first visited the Gentiles, to take out of them a people for his name. And with this the words of the prophets agree, [Acts 15:14,15]

On the day of Pentecost in Jerusalem (about 30 A.D.) a small group of Christians began to bear witness for Jesus Christ. Beginning with that event, the expansion of the Christian religion for the next three hundred years was without parallel. There is always the danger that we will excessively glorify the Christian church of the first three centuries. That we will make them into super Christians and thus very unlike us. They had divisions and weaknesses and failures just as we do. Nonetheless, that church had something that we need to recapture. There were many similarities between them and us. They had the commissionings of Christ. We have the commissionings of Christ. They had the presence of God with them. We have the presence of God with us. What was it then that the early church had that we do not have? I think it was not what they had that we do not have--but how much more we have that they did not have! They had the simple gospel of Jesus Christ without a lot of the baggage that has been accumulated along the way. And they shared that gospel.

As the church grew throughout the centuries it became more sophisticated in its understanding and awareness of theology. It distinguished differing ideas and concepts of theology. Gradually the theological understanding of the scriptures began more and more to consume the church. And as the church continued to grow in size its administration became more and more complex. In addition, no later than the fourth century it became increasingly involved in secular affairs. Gradually evangelism, which had been at the heart of the church's mission and activity, was moved aside to make room for other interests.

There are many worthy causes for the church to undertake. From the outset, the Christian community understood that its major mission was to make Jesus Christ known. They recognized that everything else was secondary (not unimportant--but second in priority). Since that first three hundred years, the church has had increasing difficulty in differentiating between its primary mission and secondary or tertiary matters. This elevating of other concerns can be understood, at times. During the period of the Protestant Reformation the concerns of the reformers had to do especially with their understanding of the nature of the church and of the doctrine of salvation. There was not always a great deal of energy left over for evangelism and world mission. Nonetheless, missionaries have been at work all through the darkest days of church history.

In the late Middle Ages, Christopher Columbus, a Roman Catholic, exhibited great missionary vision. Columbus is frequently associated with discovery--with the conquest and exploitation of the North and South American continents. Whatever the motives of some who accompanied him and of many who followed--Columbus' main objective was that people would be introduced to Jesus Christ. Too often this basic truth about Christopher Columbus has been lost. When Columbus contemplated the new world (recognizing that he did not fully understand the configuration of that new world), he dreamed of bringing the gospel to a vast region. He believed that the gospel had to be preached to the whole world before Christ would return and his kingdom be established on earth. These are the words of Christopher Columbus:

> I prayed to the most merciful Lord about my heart's great desire and he gave me the spirit and the intelligence for the task. Seafaring, astronomy, geometry, arithmetic, skill in drafting spherical maps and placing correctly the cities, rivers, mountains, and ports. I also studied cosmology, history, chronology, and philosophy. It was the Lord who put into my mind and I could feel his hand upon me to sail from here to the Indies. All who heard of my project rejected it with laughter, ridiculing me. There was no question that the inspiration was from the Holy Spirit because he comforted me with rays of marvelous illumination from the Holy Scriptures, a strong and clear testimony from the books of the Old Testament, from the four gospels and from the 23 epistles of the blessed apostles, encouraging me to continue to press forward and

without ceasing for a moment they now encourage me to make haste. [Columbus, *The Book of the Prophecies*]

Columbus first landed on an island in the West Indies. He named that island San Salvador after his Savior. And while preparing for his fourth voyage, he wrote to Pope Alexander VI asking for priests and friars to assist him in the name of the Lord Jesus to spread his name and gospel everywhere. Christopher Columbus was a layman with great vision for the kingdom of God. His vision was that the whole world might hear the gospel and become Christ's followers.

Another example of tremendous vision for Christian witness is that of the Franciscan friars who founded twenty-one missions on the west coast (now contained within the present state of California). Between 1769 and 1823 these missions were established from San Diego in the south to Sonoma in the north. Many of the names of the missions are now the names of well known cities in California such as San Diego, San Gabriel, San Luis Obispo, Santa Barbara, San Jose, Santa Clara, and Monterey. On occasion a mission may have engaged in counter productive or questionable activities. But the vision was grand in scope, to reach the western part of the new world for Jesus Christ.

The church of Jesus Christ is growing today. Much of that growth is the direct result of the modern missionary movement. That movement developed among Protestants beginning in the late 1700s. It came to flower in the 1800s and has continued to flourish in the twentieth century. In the past one hundred years the church has sprung up in many places where it was not known before. When one looks at the broad picture--the whole world--he should be impressed with the continuing growth of the Christian church. However, that growth is uneven. There has been retrogression in Western Europe. During the 1970s and 1980s the growth of the church in North America has been slight. The substantial growth of the church in Africa, South America, and Asia, where missionaries and newly developing churches have been hard at work has been substantial--sometimes dramatic. Compared to the Christian community from which they came, these missionaries have been relatively few in number--but they have evidenced tremendous concern that Christ be made known.

Let us return, in our minds, to the day of Pentecost (fifty days after the resurrection of Christ; ten days after his ascension). The book of Acts, chapter one, informs us that there were a hundred and twenty believers gathered in Jerusalem. (There were, of course, others scattered throughout Judea and Samaria and Galilee and on the east side of the Jordan in Perea and the Decapolis.) The day of Pentecost arrived, and three thousand people responded to the gospel and were added to the church in Jerusalem. A short time later, Acts 4:4 states, "But many of those who heard the word believed; and the number of the men came to about five thousand." The church spread throughout the Mediterranean world so that within one hundred years after the ascension of Christ there were Christian churches in every major city. By 300 A.D. there were at least ten million Christians. By 1600 A.D., one hundred million Christians. By the beginning of this century (1900) about 460,000,000. And by 1990, perhaps, 1,700,000,000 out of a world population of five billion. The Christian church continues to grow.

The greatest percentage of growth for the Christian church was that first three hundred years in which the church increased from the 120 persons in Jerusalem to about ten million. That growth was fired by a commitment to the centrality of evangelism. The missionary growth that continues is still inspired by a spirit of evangelism and a passion for a world knowing and obeying Jesus Christ. The challenge is tremendous. The Christian church continues to grow at about the rate of population expansion. Thus, there are increasing numbers of people without Christ. As the Christian community grows, the non-Christian community also continues to expand. Jesus said, "The fields are white unto harvest." He said, "pray therefore the Lord of the harvest to send out laborers into his harvest." (Luke 10:2) In spite of spectacular growth of the church in Asia in the twentieth century, only one person in twenty-two of that continent is a professing Christian. And there are countries like Saudi Arabia, Nepal, and Afghanistan where the gospel of Christ is scarcely known.

God's focus is on the entire world. Jesus' final commissioning is stated in Acts 1:8, "You shall be my witnesses in Jerusalem, in Judea, in Samaria and unto the uttermost parts of the earth." Jerusalem is where they began. Judea was the nearby--proximate area. Samaria was farther to the north. From those areas the scope

Evangelism and World Mission

was limitless. Jesus envisioned the gospel spreading to the entire earth. In the same manner, Christians are to look out from their cities and counties and states and visualize the need of the whole world for the gospel.

God called Abram and said, "I will bless those who bless you, and him who curses you I will curse; and by you all the families of the earth will be blessed." [Genesis 12:3] He called a man at a particular time and place--but through him he was looking at the whole world. John 3:16 proclaims, "God so loved the world". Jesus commanded, "Go therefore and make disciples of all nations." Again and again we have the emphasis in scripture that the believing community is to be concerned to share the good news of God both to neighbors and to the whole world. It is through the church that these commissionings of Jesus Christ can be fulfilled. Because one person cannot be in Chicago, in New Orleans, in Brussels, or in Bangkok all at the same time. Through the work and the ministry of the whole church, cooperating and working together, all Christians can be involved in world-wide witness and mission. Our primary responsibility is to share the good news of Jesus Christ with others.

Here are four motives for evangelism and world mission that we derive from the scriptures: <u>The first is the authority of Jesus Christ</u>. He said that we are to be his witnesses. Many may well prefer those passages in the Bible that speak of the love and the forgiveness of God and of the wonderful salvation that they find in Jesus Christ. But the same Bible also gives the emphatic words of our Savior that we are to be his witnesses; that we are to be involved in sharing the good news both here and throughout the world. Jesus Christ is the head of the church.

> Therefore God has highly exalted him and bestowed on him the name which is above every name, that at the name of Jesus every knee should bow in heaven and on earth and under the earth and every tongue confess that Jesus Christ is Lord to the glory of God the Father.
> [Philippians 2:9-11]

By the authority of this Christ, who is Lord and head of the church, all believers are to be witnesses for him. Through the ministry of the church and worthwhile Christian agencies, and through personal encounter with other people these gracious commissionings of our Savior can be fulfilled.

A second motive for evangelism and world mission is the love of God. The apostle Paul wrote, "For the love of Christ controls us". (II Corinthians 5:14) He went on to affirm that we are ambassadors for Christ. He was bound by the love of God (God's love for him and God's love for others). As one grasps the depth of that love--he should be moved to be generous in sharing what he has received. We have been loved. Now God wants to love others through us.

Ephesians 2:4,5, states:

> God who is rich in mercy, out of the great love with which he loved us, even when we were dead through our trespasses, made us alive together with Christ.

The love of God should impel one to be personally involved in sharing the good news of Jesus Christ.

A third motive for evangelism is what Jesus Christ has done personally for those who believe in him. If one has believed in Christ, he has been forgiven of his sins, he is heir to a vast eternal inheritance, and he has begun to experience God's fuller blessing in his life. If one has received and experienced God's goodness in such generous measure, then he should surely want others to know that goodness as well. It is a shame to have good news and not tell others about it!

A fourth motivating factor for personal involvement in evangelism and world mission is the need of other people. People have a variety of needs: physical health and well being, food, shelter and clothing, a sense of worthwhileness, that they are accepted by others, and they have spiritual needs. Spiritual needs are not necessarily the most keenly felt. Nor are they always perceived to be of top priority--but their neglect or distortion can be the most debilitating to the individual in the long run. God is the author of life, the sustainer of life, and the claimer of life. Sooner or later life begins to unravel for those who do not recognize God as most significant to their lives. The symptoms can be severe. But without help people may not recognize where the cure is to be found.

I am not claiming that after people are converted to Jesus Christ everyone will be free from all problems. Christians must grow in grace. They have to learn obedience to Christ. And all who affirm faith in Christ have not learned that obedience! Many who identify themselves as Christians are not growing in grace as they ought to. Nonetheless, the true needs of people and society cannot be met without Jesus Christ. Our recognition of the needs of others should move us to share our faith with them.

All people are accountable before God. They stand under his inevitable judgment. Without Christ they face a desperate eternity. The Christian should be moved out of compassion to warn, exhort, and encourage those without Christ to believe in him lest they experience fearful consequences.

What should the Christian do in response to this major emphasis in the Bible? All Christians should consider themselves directly involved in the world-wide Christian mission. You may feel that your part is insignificant. It takes many bricks to build a building, and which brick is insignificant? Every Christian should recognize that God has some task for him or her to fulfill in that worldwide mission.

Christian witness is about Jesus Christ, but it is accomplished by people. There is a great church in Korea today because missionaries went to Korea in the late 1800s. Prepare yourself to be a more active witness for Jesus Christ. Weekday Bible studies provide an excellent means in growing in knowledge of the Bible and in one's ability to talk about what one believes. Many churches offer specific training programs in evangelism. Avail yourself of those programs or studies that will help you to have more freedom in sharing your faith. If one knows that on some occasion he will be thrown in the water--he ought to learn to swim!

Every Christian can select a country, a geographic area, and/or a mission agency and make it a focus of his attention and learning. In addition to other prayer concerns, the Christian should be praying for another person, that he knows and has contact with, to come to Christ--and he should pray daily for at least one missionary.

The issue, then, is more of what one is ready to give than of gifts, skills, or resources that he may possess. We read that Jesus observed a variety of people coming to the temple and contributing their funds to the treasury. Some people made large impressive contributions. A widow put in only a mite, which was the smallest coin made. Jesus commended her because she had given everything that she had. What seems small in our sight may be great in God's sight. In John, chapter six, we read of the feeding of the five thousand men (besides women and children). The multitude had been with Jesus all day, and Jesus felt that they should be fed. Andrew brought a young boy to Jesus who had five barley loaves and two fish. The disciples were not so different from many of us. They did not see how Jesus could do it. The boy had a very small amount of food compared to the need. But Jesus fed the multitude, and after everyone had eaten as much as they wanted they filled twelve baskets with the left over food. They brought Jesus what they had. He did the rest!

We cannot change hearts and lives. We may not even be able to convince people. But we can bear witness to the one whom we know. And Jesus can do great things with that kind of obedience. In the words of Paul, "I planted, Apollos watered, but God gave the growth."

Further Reading

    Columbus, Christopher, *The Book of the Prophecies*
    Green, Michael, *Evangelism in the Early Church*, Eerdmans
    Schaller, Lyle E., *It's A Different World*, Abingdon
    Trueblood, Elton, *The Incendiary Fellowship*, Harper & Row
    Winter, Ralph D. and Hawthorne, Steven C., *Perspectives on the World Christian Movement*, William Carey Library

For Reflection or Discussion

1. What is the main business of the church?

2. What are some other important things that the church is

called to do?

3. What is the major obstacle to Christian witness for you personally?

4. What do you think is the major motivating factor for Christian witness and missions?

CHAPTER SEVENTEEN
PRINCIPLES OF JUSTICE AND COMPASSION

> And he said to him, "you shall love the Lord your God with all your heart, and with all you soul, and with all your mind. This is the great and first commandment. And a second is like it, You shall love your neighbor as yourself. On these two commandments depend all the law and the prophets. [Matthew 22:37-40]

> So whatever you wish that men would do to you, do so to them; for this is the law and the prophets. [Matthew 7:12]

> Do nothing from selfishness or conceit, but in humility count others better than yourselves. Let each of you look not only to his own interests, but also to the interests of others. [Philippians 2:3,4]

For many, the heart of Christianity is personal salvation: the individual believing in Christ and entering into an eternal relationship with God. But for other Christians the central matter is the impact that the church can make upon the institutions of society. They see hungry people, a need for adequate housing, people who are the victims of racial prejudice, exploitive business practices, the terrible threat of nuclear warfare, and a plethora of other concerns. It seems to them that the primary calling of the Christian is to do all that can be done to ameliorate the suffering and confront the injustices in this world.

The Bible makes it plain that God is concerned with the welfare of all persons. He demands righteousness of the nations, and promises to them his blessings if they will pursue righteousness. And he warns them of his certain judgment if they disregard him and practice injustice. What is the proper role for the individual Christian and for the church when confronted with the massive needs of persons and of society? Who sets the priorities for our individual and corporate ministries? Surely we work out the details and make the up-to-date applications, but Jesus Christ remains the head of the church. We are his servants; he is our Lord and Master. To the degree that he gives us direction and leadership--we are to follow him. If we set the rules, without due regard for God, we are not faithful servants. The pursuit of justice, without any regard for God, is manifestation of practical atheism; and is doomed to disappointment, frustration, and failure. The Bible makes it clear that God is the sovereign authority. The basic rules come from him.

Throughout the entire history of the Christian Church, the Christian community has generally agreed that not only should the individual Christian be concerned for justice, but the church itself should exhibit active concern in matters of righteousness. There are appropriate times when the church must speak what it believes and should confront what it recognizes to be wrong. However, Christians do not always agree regarding issues that should be dealt with nor as to the depth of involvement. How then are genuine concerns to be properly addressed?

Some American denominations have become improperly and excessively involved in social issues. At times they have become engaged with so many issues that they have not been able to give sufficient or adequate attention to any one of them. Their total involvement in the area of social concern becomes so extensive that their basic responsibilities in evangelism and world missions are neglected. One factor to be considered, in entering the arena of social concern, is the availability of resources of time, energy, personnel, and money that can be realistically committed to any given cause. How much will involvement in one area detract from the fulfilling of important responsibilities in another area? All operate within the limitations of time, energy, and precious resources. Jesus warned,

> For which of you, desiring to build a tower, does not first sit down and count the cost, whether he has enough to complete it? Otherwise when he has laid a foundation, and is not able to finish, all who see it begin to mock him saying, 'This man began to build, and was not able to finish.' [Luke 14:28-30]

There are, without question, occasions when the Christian community should publicly confront what is wrong and unrighteous in society. Some current areas would include serious occasions of racial injustice, world hunger, hard core pornography, child abuse, abortion, the drug traffic, and homelessness.

The Major Themes of the Bible

I. SOME FOUNDATIONAL PRINCIPLES

Let us deal with some of the foundational principles that the Bible gives regarding righteousness, justice, goodness, compassion, and mercy.

1. <u>First, God is our authority: our basic directions must come from him</u>. Great peace comes to one's life as one effectively recognizes and willingly accepts God's sovereign authority. If there is any secret to inner peace and deliverance from inner psychological turmoil--it is the ability to recognize that God is God and there is no other! The distresses of the world should not provoke an undue anxiety in the child of God. After all, our basic concepts of righteousness and justice come from the Bible. The Bible must, therefore, provide the basic foundation and structure for social justice concerns. We must not get beyond God in this matter.

2. <u>The Bible teaches that God is absolutely pure, absolutely holy--he is perfect in his righteousness and his justice</u>. Sentiment on the side of compassion and goodness is not sufficient. The believer must be an active participant. On his final journey to Jerusalem, while passing through Jericho, Jesus encountered Zacchaeus. Because he was a short man and not able to see over the crowd, Zacchaeus had climbed up into a sycamore tree in order to see Jesus. Jesus stopped, and looking up at Zacchaeus told him to come down from the tree, and that he was going to have dinner at his house that day. Later on, at his house, Zacchaeus proclaimed his belief in Christ, and he said,

> Behold, Lord, the half of my goods I give to the poor; and if I have defrauded anyone of anything, I restore it fourfold. [Luke 19:8]

Jesus commended Zacchaeus, saying, "Today salvation has come to this house,". Zacchaeus acted on his belief.

> My children, love must not be a matter of words or talk, it must be genuine, and show itself in action.
> [I John 3:18, NEB]

Jesus told the parable of the Good Samaritan. A person, who had been robbed and beaten was left by the side of the road to die. His plight was seen by a number of individuals, some of whom were actively practicing their religion. But they turned their heads and kept on going without offering any assistance. A Samaritan came along and rescued the man; binding his wounds, caring for him, and providing for his continuing care. Righteousness is more that avoiding evil. It is being active in doing what is good and right. Jesus set forth the Good Samaritan as an example of what it means to love one's neighbor. In doing so he greatly expanded the bounds of one's neighborhood!

In Matthew, chapter 25, Jesus spoke of the day of judgment when the Messiah will sit upon his throne and the nations will be gathered before him. He said that the sheep would be put on his right and the goats on his left. He will say to those on his right:

> Come, O blessed of my Father, inherit the kingdom prepared for you from the foundation of the world; for I was hungry and you gave me food, I was thirsty and you gave me drink. I was a stranger and you welcomed me. I was naked and you clothed me. I was sick and you visited me. I was in prison and you came to me.   [Matthew 25:34-36]

He commends the sheep, not for what they avoided doing, but for what they did. Justice and righteousness, in a biblical sense, has to do with active compassion and correction of evil.

II. THE BIBLE CLEARLY DECLARES GOD'S CONCERN FOR JUSTICE AND COMPASSION

> He has showed you, O man, what is good; and what does the Lord require of you but to do justice, and to love kindness, and to walk humbly with your God?   [Micah 6:8]

> Thus says the Lord: Keep justice and do righteousness, for soon my salvation will come and my deliverance be revealed.   [Isaiah 56:1]

> Is not this the fast that I choose: to loose the bonds of wickedness, to undo the thongs of the yoke, to let the oppressed go free, and to break every yoke? Is it not to share your bread with the hungry, and bring the homeless poor into your house; when you see the naked to cover him, and not to hide yourself from your own flesh?
> [Isaiah 58:6,7]

> Righteousness and justice are the foundation of thy throne; steadfast love and faithfulness go before thee.
> [Psalm 89:14]

The above passages, and others included in this chapter, are only a few from many more that could be cited. (1) Righteousness in dealing with others, (2) compassion for others, and (3) dealing with injustice are not peripheral issues with Almighty God. They are central concerns. They must, therefore, be received as of great importance to those who love God. Righteousness in dealing with others is the most immediate and in a sense the easiest for us to handle. We are not to take advantage of others. We are to deal with others honestly, fairly, and kindly. Most of us have to learn compassion. We do not practice it naturally. The cruelty, meanness, and deliberate unkindnesses that are all around remind us of our own limitations and insufficiencies. But we can reach out to others. We can care for others. In a very real sense the person whom we can help is a real opportunity for us. He or she is a gift of God giving opportunity to minister in his name.

Correcting injustice is the most difficult of the three factors mentioned above. This presents an arena that ordinarily cannot be handled by a single individual. The believer needs the company, the cooperation, the help of others. And he must be well informed. One needs to be as sure as possible that he is not aiming at the wrong target. We need to make very sure that any corrective measures we undertake do not do more harm than good. That our motive is not vindictive--but that we have a genuine desire to enable improvement; to set an example, to establish precedents, that will contribute to greater fairness and justice in the future. Those who seek to correct societal injustices need a good measure of humility regarding their own shortcomings. Ordinarily, corrective actions will be undertaken by a minority; frequently a small group. But there should be a sense in the Christian community as a whole that this is the right thing to do. If genuine Christians are evenly divided over an issue, or if most Christians are opposed to a course of action, which is presumably designed to correct some injustice, then those who propose that course of action should be given pause.

III. BIBLICAL PRINCIPLES OF JUSTICE AND RIGHTEOUSNESS

There are at least eight important biblical foundation stones of justice and righteousness:

1. Truth. God is a God of truth. Jesus always spoke the truth. The disciples affirmed the truth of the gospel that they proclaimed. Jesus said to his adversaries that they spoke lies because they were of their father, the devil, who is characteristically a liar.

> For he comes to judge the earth. He will judge the world with righteousness and the peoples with his truth.
> [Psalm 96:13]

> O Lord do not thy eyes look for truth? [Jeremiah 5:3]

> Jesus then said to the Jews who had believed in him, "If you continue in my word, you are truly my disciples, and you will know the truth, and the truth will make you free."
> [John 8:31,32]

Television has enabled us to watch many Congressional hearings over the years including those associated with Watergate and the so called Irangate/Contra Hearings. In 1988 millions witnessed the penetrating examinations of Colonel Oliver North, Robert McFarland, Admiral Poindexter, and others. We also follow with interest the political campaigns of those seeking their party's nomination in the presidential years. What is the point? Almost everyone affirms the importance of the truth! The purpose of judicial process--the aim of the Congressional committees is to ferret out the truth. An important function of the political campaign process is to sweat out the truth about the candidates.

People may be careless about the truth; they may even excuse a certain laxity regarding the truth in their own lives. But they want the truth from others! To the degree that we do not have the truth, personal relationships break down and society is undermined. God is a God of truth, and those who are associated with him are to be people of truth. Jesus said, "let your yea be yea and your nay be nay". The work of God is not advanced by clandestine, underhanded, or dishonest practices.

2. Impartiality. A basic and integral aspect of justice is even-handedness. The law is applied equally to everyone within its

purview. The judicial processes are open to all regardless of their race, class, ability, or status in society. Justice is blindfolded; she applies the law equally to all. This principle of justice is stated many times in scripture:

> There shall be one law for the native and for the stranger who sojourns among you. [Exodus 12:49]

> But you shall keep my statutes and my ordinances and do none of these abominations, either the native or the stranger who sojourns among you [Leviticus 18:26]

> For the assembly, there shall be one statute for you and for the stranger who sojourns with you, a perpetual statute throughout your generations; as you are, so shall the sojourner be before the Lord. One law and one ordinance shall be for you and for the stranger who sojourns with you. [Numbers 15:15,16]

3. <u>Honest Business Transactions</u>; Just Weights and Balances. One of the significant ways that God's desire for honesty and integrity is expressed is in terms of just weights and balances. If the butcher says that he is giving a pound of meat, God expects him to give a pound of meat--not less. If the merchant tells you that he is giving you two yards of material of a certain quality, God expects him to give you the two yards, that he has promised, and not something short of that.

> You shall do no wrong in judgment, in measures of length or weight or quantity. You shall have just balances, just weights, a just ephah, and a just hin: I am the Lord your God, who brought you out of the land of Egypt. And you shall observe all my statutes and all my ordinances, and do them: I am the Lord. [Leviticus 19:35,36]

God approves of honest merchants and honest business people. He will judge the dishonest and the unjust, "Shall I acquit the man with wicked scales and with a bag of deceitful weights?" (Micah 6:11)

4. <u>The protection of property rights</u>. The Bible does not endorse the unlimited acquisition of wealth. Quite the contrary. The Old Testament system put stringent limits on the acquisition of wealth

by protecting family property rights and forbidding the lending of money at interest. I do not mean to say that the lending of money at interest is always wrong. I am simply making the point that God restricted the acquisition of wealth. In addition, the Bible teaches a special responsibility on the part of those who have wealth to give compassionate aid to those in need.

Fortune Magazine, The Wall Street Journal, and other publications publish annual lists of top executive salaries in the United States. There is no question but that the salaries and related compensation of top executives is excessive. The same, of course, is true for many celebrities in the entertainment and sports worlds. The Bible neither countenances nor encourages the great disparities of wealth in North America and in the rest of the world.

The Old Testament sets forth principles of property rights and wealth that remain valid. These underlying principles have not been abrogated.

After the people of Israel entered into the land of Caanan, under the leadership of Joshua, the land was distributed to the tribes and then to the clans and then to the families within those tribes. God provided a system to protect those property rights. Every fifty years there was to be a year of jubilee. Property could not be sold or obligated beyond that year. At the year of jubilee any property that had been sold or otherwise encumbered reverted to the family from which it had come. No loans could be entered into that extended beyond the year of jubilee. With the arrival of the year of jubilee all contractual obligations came to an end. Without this provision, God realized that the land would end up in fewer and fewer hands, and that was not his will.

We read in I Kings, chapter 21, of the episode of King Ahab of Israel and Naboth, a small landowner. Ahab coveted Naboth's vineyard that was near to his palace in Jezreel. Ahab offered to trade a better piece of property for Naboth's vineyard or to buy it from him for cash. Naboth refused, because it was family property. He recognized that to sell the vineyard would be to break a legitimate trust that was ultimately God-given. Ahab's wife, Jezebel, arranged for false charges to be brought against Naboth. He was tried on trumped up charges, and then taken outside of the city and stoned to death. Ahab then took possession of Naboth's vineyard. The prophet, Elijah, confronted Ahab, and

The Major Themes of the Bible

warned him of the judgment that God would bring upon him and Jezebel because they had not respected Naboth's rights. The protection of legitimate property rights is a part of God's justice. Both greed and injustice and condemned.

5. Care and compassion for the widow, the orphan, the foreigner, and the helpless.

> Wash yourselves; make yourselves clean; remove the evil of your doings from before my eyes; cease to do evil, learn to do good; seek justice, correct oppression; defend the fatherless, plead for the widow. [Isaiah 1:16,17]

The prophets especially emphasize God's concern for those who are weak and helpless in society. Those who love God are to be actively concerned for the orphan and the widow and those who need justice. The concern of many Christians for the unborn, the more than one million lives that are destroyed by abortion every year in the United States, is in harmony with these biblical mandates. God is concerned for the weakest and the helpless in society.

> Thus says the Lord: Do justice and righteousness, and deliver from the hand of the oppressor him who has been robbed. And do no wrong or violence to the alien, the fatherless, and the widow, nor shed innocent blood in this place. [Jeremiah 22:3]

> Give justice to the weak and the fatherless; maintain the right of the afflicted and the destitute. [Psalm 82:3]

Sometimes societies are irritated by and hostile to persons of foreign origin in their midst. The Christian community is to show love and concern and welcome for such persons. The widow and the orphan are properly a special responsibility of the Christian community. The church should be in the forefront of those seeking to help the homeless and the destitute.

6. Peace. Jesus said, "Blessed are the peacemakers". It would be out of keeping with the context, in which that statement was made, to suppose that his primary focus was on those who engage in international negotiations. But peace is the will of God for every level of life. It is to be a reality in the heart of every per-

son. Peace is to be a reality in the relationship of husbands and wives, within families, in churches, and in all institutions and groups that make up society. In one of the grand statements regarding the Messiah we read,

> For to us a child is born, to us a son is given; and the government will be upon his shoulder, and his name will be called "Wonderful Counselor, Mighty God, Everlasting Father, Prince of Peace". Of the increase of his government and of peace there will be no end, upon the throne of David, and over his kingdom, to establish it, and to uphold it with justice and with righteousness from this time forth and for evermore. [Isaiah 9:6,7]

The prophet Micah said,

> He shall judge between many peoples, and shall decide for strong nations afar off; and they shall beat their swords into plowshares, and their spears into pruning hooks; nation shall not lift up sword against nation, neither shall they learn war any more; but they shall sit every man under his vine and under his fig tree, and none shall make them afraid; for the mouth of the Lord of hosts has spoken.
> [Micah 4:3,4]

One day, peace at all levels will be a reality, because God's rule will be fully established. In the meantime his people are to model peace and to promote peace. Christians will not be credible in advocacy for international peace unless they exhibit it in the lesser spheres in which they are more intimately involved.

7. <u>Keeping the commandments of God</u>. We must recognize that God has a claim upon our lives--that we live in covenant relationship with him--that he has a will and a purpose that we are to adhere to. We are to obey the commandments--the laws--the precepts of scripture. Jesus closely associated authentic love for him with observance of the law of God.

> He who has my commandments and keeps them, he it is who loves me; and he who loves me will be loved by my Father, and I will love him and manifest myself to him.
> [John 14:21]

The commandments and ordinances of God are for our well-being. By keeping them, we find peace and harmony and happiness. To the degree that we disregard them, life will fall short of what God intends it to be. One cannot legitimately contend for God's will in one area and ignore or deny it in another.

8. Judgment. Judgment is a foundational principle. There are accounts to be rendered. God calls all people to live responsibly. He is not indifferent to irresponsible behavior. Belief in God and obedience to God are not options to be followed when it is convenient. The consequences for unbelief and disregard for God are ultimate. To some people, the judgment of God seems unbelievable and unacceptable. People compare themselves with one another. Human myopia causes us either not to see or to distort the fact of God's judgment; we are too close to the problem; too much a part of the problem. But God is above us. His thoughts are not our thoughts neither are his ways our ways [Isaiah 55:8,9]. He is a holy God, and he judges people by his perfect standards of holiness. Therefore, all need recourse to the cross of Christ. All need to personally accept deliverance from God's judgment through Jesus Christ. Those who think that they can prevail against the judgment of God without trusting in Christ are tragically mistaken.

> Therefore the wicked will not stand in the judgment, nor sinners in the congregation of the righteous; for the Lord knows the way of the righteous, but the way of the wicked will perish. [Psalm 1:5,6]

> And there is salvation in no one else, for there is no other name under heaven given among men by which we must be saved. [Acts 4:12]

God did not set forth his laws so that people may observe them when they are inclined to do so. He is God. His will is to be obeyed. God is concerned with common justice--honest business practices--the avoidance of violence--speaking the truth--compassion for the hurting. His concern will evidence itself in absolute rectitude. Judgment is integral to righteousness--otherwise righteousness is reduced to a divine sentiment.

In the early 1960s a leader in the ecumenical movement popularized a phrase, "Mickey Mouse Morality". What he evidently meant was that the Christian community should be involved with great issues of justice and not concern itself with petty matters such as personal standards of morality. From a biblical standpoint the two cannot be divided. Big houses are made out of little bricks. The Bible declares, "whatever a man sows, that he will also reap" [Galatians 6:7]. Those who desire righteousness and goodness on a major scale must work for it in every area.

This is not to say that our final hope is in ourselves individually or corporately. We, of course, should do our best, and all of us are capable of better than we do. Our ultimate hope for justice, righteousness, and peace is in Christ, in his return, and in his kingdom. One of the great gifts that God has given to us is that he has involved us in his enterprise that we might share the good news of Jesus Christ with others, that we might live for him, and that we might further the work of his kingdom. Our prayers, our giving, and our living are intertwined with the return of Christ and the establishment of his kingdom.

Further Reading
The Book of Amos
Matthew 25:31-46
Luke 10:25-37
Lovelace, Richard F., *Dynamics of Spiritual Life,* Chapter 12, "The Spiritual Roots of Christian Social Concern", Inter-Varsity Press

For Reflection or Discussion

1. Are there issues of injustice in your local area that the Christian community should be involved with?

2. Where is the balance between humility: a recognition of our own flaws and limitations--and not being immobilized so that we are effectively engaged in caring for people and in justice concerns?

3. Give instances on the national or international level--
   a. where Christians have incorrectly gotten involved
   b. where Christians have properly gotten involved or should have

4. What can the individual Christian do to correct major areas of injustice?

CHAPTER EIGHTEEN

THE RETURN OF CHRIST AND ENSUING EVENTS

The Old Testament speaks abundantly of the return of Christ. But there is little distinction between his first and second advents. Many Old Testament messianic passages speak of or allude to the Messiah as one who is to suffer, and quite explicitly in Isaiah 52:13-53:12, that the Messiah is to suffer for the sins of the people. Thus, there is an apparent conflict between the passages that speak of the glory and exaltation of the Messiah and those that speak of his humiliation and suffering. This apparent conflict is resolved in the New Testament as we realize that what must have appeared to many readers of the Old Testament to be a single messianic event was in fact two events: the humble birth of Jesus by the Virgin Mary and his return as reigning king of the universe at the end of the age.

If we think about the tumultuous welcome of Jesus when he entered Jerusalem on Palm Sunday, we can understand that those who identified Jesus as the Messiah must well have expected him to manifest himself as an exalted ruler. We can understand the puzzlement of the disciples when immediately prior to Jesus' ascension they asked, "Lord, will you at this time restore the kingdom to Israel?" [Acts 1:6] Jesus' response to them clearly indicated another time; a future event. If there was any doubt, it was made plain by the two angels who spoke to the disciples immediately after the ascension of Jesus,

> Men of Galilee, why do you stand looking into heaven? This Jesus, who was taken up from you into heaven, will come in the same way as you saw him go into heaven.
> [Acts 1:11]

Many of the Old Testament messianic passages await their fulfillment in the second advent of Jesus Christ. Thus, they supply a rich resource for our understanding of that marvelous climactic event of history. With many related passages in the New Testament they underscore that, indeed, the second coming of Christ is a major biblical theme.

The Return of Christ and Ensuing Events

Jesus emphasized his return and its immense significance, and the remainder of the New Testament gives it a central place. In the words of the apostle Paul, it is a "blessed hope".

> awaiting our blessed hope, the appearing of the glory of our great God and Savior Jesus Christ, [Titus 2:13]

The major passage in the gospels having to do with the second coming of Christ is found in Matthew 24:3-25:46. Shortened versions of the same discourse are found in Mark 13:1-27 and Luke 21:5-36. Although the Luke passage is considerably shorter than that in Matthew, it gives some additional material relating to the return of the Lord that is not found in Matthew. Additional important passages regarding the return of the Lord are as follows:

I Corinthians 11:26
I Thessalonians 4:13-5:11
II Thessalonians 1:5-10
II Thessalonians 2:1-12
II Peter 3:3-13
Hebrews 9:28
Revelation 1:7

However, there are many other New Testament passages that refer to the return of Christ or infer that return.

Relying especially on Matthew 24:3-25:46 and supplementing with other New Testament passages on the return of Christ, let us set forth those truths that are clearly taught:

I. THE PLAIN TEACHINGS OF THE NEW TESTAMENT REGARDING THE RETURN OF CHRIST

1. <u>The return of Christ will be unexpected by many</u>. The precise time of Christ's return will not be known to any on Earth. But for many it will come as a complete and unwelcome surprise. "There will be weeping and gnashing of teeth." However, many who believe in him will be prepared and ready. They may be surprised, but they will not be taken unaware. The parables of the five wise and the five foolish young maidens and of the man who entrusted his property to his servants (Matthew, chapter 25) portray the situation in which some will be ready for their master's

return and others will not.

2. <u>The return of Christ is an event to be anticipated and desired for those who believe in Christ.</u>

> awaiting our blessed hope, the appearing of the glory of our great God and Savior Jesus Christ, [Titus 2:13]

> I tell you I shall not drink again of this fruit of the vine until that day when I drink it new with you in my Father's kingdom. [Matthew 26:29]

> Now when these things begin to take place, look up and raise your heads, because your redemption is drawing near. [Luke 21:28]

> Our Lord, come! [I Corinthians 16:22]

The salvation which the believer has sought will begin to reach its fulfillment at the return of Christ.

3. <u>The return of Christ will be preceded by a time of tribulation.</u> I fully realize that many fine Christians believe that there will be a "rapture" of the church prior to a time of tribulation. It may well be an appealing doctrine, but it is not what the scriptures teach. Matthew 24:29-31 is quite explicit:

> Immediately after the tribulation of those days the sun will be darkened, and the moon will not give its light, and the stars will fall from heaven, and the powers of the heavens will be shaken; then will appear the sign of the Son of man in heaven, and then all the tribes the earth will mourn, and they will see the Son of man coming on the clouds of heaven with power and great glory; and he will send out his angels with a loud trumpet call, and they will gather his elect from the four winds, from one end of heaven to the other.

I recognize that other passages of scripture are referred to by those who teach a "pre-tribulation rapture", but that idea is based on an unnecessary interpretation. When interpretation comes up against a clear and definite statement like that above, it must give way. Again I recognize that a case is made that only a select group of believers will experience this tribulation period. But when Jesus spoke of the time of tribulation he spoke of its effects in a general sense and, indeed, indicated that for the sake of the elect the time would be shortened. It can be argued that "the elect" refers to a very limited and specific group of believers, but the most natural reading is that it encompasses all believers.

Many students of scripture recognize that Jesus warnings of a time of tribulation had a dual focus: the destruction of Jerusalem by the Roman armies in 70 A.D. and a time of dreadful and devastating events prior to his second coming. If that is so, the first warning regarding the destruction of Jerusalem was quite clearly a general warning. Taken in the same context, the warning of a second time of suffering would also be general.

While I believe it is plain that the Bible speaks of a convulsive period prior to the return of Christ, an excessive zeal to exempt believers from tribulation misreads scripture in another sense. Christians down through history, including the present time, have endured all kinds of suffering for their Savior. Jesus warned all who believe in him that they may suffer ostracism, division in their families, harassment, psychological and physical abuse, and even death for his sake. Faithfulness to Christ has meant deliverance in these tribulations rather than deliverance from them.

4. <u>The return of Christ will be preceded and accompanied by cosmic signs</u>.
    a. The sun will be darkened
    b. the moon will not give its light
    c. the stars will fall from heaven
    d. the powers of the heavens will be shaken
    e. there will be an unusual display of waves and roaring in the oceans and seas

5. <u>The return of Christ will occur in such a manner that all will know of it. It will be accompanied by certain definite signs</u>.

> Then if any one says to you, 'Lo, here is the Christ! or 'There he is!' do not believe it. For false Christs and false prophets will arise and show great signs and wonders, so as to lead astray, if possible, even the elect. Lo, I have told you beforehand. So, if they say to you, 'Lo, he is in the wilderness,' do not go out; if they say, 'Lo, he is in the

> inner rooms,' do not believe it. For as the lightning comes from the east and shines as far as the west, so will be the coming of the Son of man. [Matthew 24:23-27]

> then will appear the sign of the Son of man in heaven, ..., and they will see the Son of man coming on the clouds of heaven with power and great glory; and he will send out his angels with a loud trumpet call, [Matthew 24:30,31]

> For the Lord himself will descend from heaven with a cry of command, with the archangel's call, and with the sound of the trumpet of God. [I Thessalonians 4:16]

6. A powerful figure of evil will appear on the earth before the return of Christ.

> when you see the desolating sacrilege spoken of by the prophet Daniel, standing in the holy place [Matthew 24:15]

> Let no one deceive you in any way; for that day will not come, unless the rebellion comes first, and the man of lawlessness is revealed, the son of perdition, who opposes and exalts himself against every so-called god or object of worship, so that he takes his seat in the temple of God, proclaiming himself to be God. [II Thessalonians 2:3,4]

> And then the lawless one will be revealed, and the Lord Jesus will slay him with the breath of his mouth and destroy him by his appearing and his coming. The coming of the lawless one by the activity of Satan will be with all power and with pretended signs and wonders, and with all wicked deception for those who are to perish, because they refused to love the truth and so be saved.
> [II Thessalonians 2:8-10]

> Children, it is the last hour; and as you have heard that antichrist is coming, so now many antichrists have come; therefore we know that it is the last hour. [I John 2:18]

> And the beast was captured, and with it the false prophet who in its presence had worked the signs by which he deceived those who had received the mark of the beast and those who worshiped its image. [Revelation 19:20]

II. WHEN CHRIST COMES WHAT WILL HAPPEN? WHAT WILL BE THE SEQUENCE OF EVENTS?

As we seek to deal with those events that will accompany and follow the return of Christ, Deuteronomy 29:29 is very helpful:

> The secret things belong to the Lord our God; but the things that are revealed belong to us and to our children for ever,

I do not want to be dogmatic about these matters. I believe that the Bible gives us a sequence of events, and I intend to set them forth. However, I am quite aware that this is an area of substantial controversy among Christians. When we begin putting a number of passages of scripture together, differing arrangements by different people are inevitable. We are dealing with a future realm that is as yet unknown to us. It is quite possible that in this area, especially, we err in making figurative language literal an literal language figurative. Nonetheless, I believe that I owe it to the reader to set forth what I believe the Bible says about the sequence of events following the return of Christ. The following order is based primarily on Revelation, chapters 20 and 21:

1. <u>The resurrection of the just</u> (the first resurrection)

2. <u>The millennial reign of Christ</u>. In one sense the idea of a reign of Christ on earth for one thousand years is supported only by a single passage in the Bible, Revelation 20:1-10. However, the idea of the earth under the reign of the Messiah is explicit in many Old Testament passages. I recognize that some rationalize these passages as typological or symbolic of heaven. However, if they are typological that would support the idea of an earthly millennium (the millennium would be the type of which heaven is the antitype). Ordinarily the type precedes the greater reality that it represents.

> The wolf shall dwell with the lamb, and the leopard shall lie down with the kid, and the calf and the lion and the fatling together, and a little child shall lead them. The cow and the bear shall feed; their young shall lie down together; and the lion shall eat straw like the ox. The sucking child shall play over the hole of the asp, and the weaned child shall put his hand on the adder's den. They

> shall not hurt or destroy in all my holy mountain; for the earth shall be full of the knowledge of the Lord as the waters cover the sea. [Isaiah 11:6-9]
>
> It shall come to pass in the latter days that the mountain of the house of the Lord shall be established as the highest of the mountains, and shall be raised up above the hills; and peoples shall flow to it, and many nations shall come, and say: "Come, let us go up to the mountain of the Lord, to the house of the God of Jacob; that he may teach us his ways and we may walk in his paths." For out of Zion shall go forth the law, and the word of the Lord from Jerusalem. He shall judge between many peoples, and shall decide for strong nations afar off; and they shall beat their swords into plowshares, and their spears into pruning hooks; nation shall not lift up sword against nation, neither shall they learn war any more; but they shall sit every man under his vine and under his fig tree, and none shall make them afraid; [Micah 4:1-4]

Many take the above and similar passages as symbolic of heaven. However, these passages seem to speak very much of the earth. It is fitting that life on earth be completed with a righteous and blessed reign of the Messiah prior to a new heaven and a new earth. The many passages that refer to the Messiah as the successor of king David find their initial fulfillment in an earthly reign of Christ.

Christians who care about the doctrines relating to the return of Christ can be divided into three groups:

    a. Post-millennial: the belief that a golden age of the kingdom of God will be achieved on earth through the proclamation of the gospel, the conversion of growing numbers to Jesus Christ, the faithful obedience of Christians, and the growing influence of the teachings of Christ upon all society. The return of Christ will then occur at the culmination of this golden age.

    b. Pre-millennial: the belief that Christ will return to earth at an unexpected time and establish his kingdom on earth for a period of one thousand years prior to the culmination of all things and a new heaven and a new earth.

c. A-millennial: the idea of a milennial kingdom is spiritualized. The milennial kingdom (or the golden age) are symbols of heaven. When Christ returns, the new age will commence in heaven, not on earth.

3. <u>Following the one thousand year reign of Christ Satan will be loosed and he will deceive the nations.</u>

4. <u>Gog and Magog will gather for battle.</u> Fire will come down from heaven and will consume them.

5. <u>The devil will be thrown into the lake of fire.</u>

6. <u>The resurrection of the unjust</u> (The second resurrection).

7. <u>The great white throne judgment.</u>

8. <u>A new heaven and a new earth.</u>

Having set forth the above sequence of events as properly derived from the Bible, let us clearly state that the essential truth is that Christ will return to Earth. He will establish his kingdom and judge the unrighteous. Those who believe in him will be endowed with new bodies and enjoy the blessedness and glory of God forever. Further details are intriguing, but at some point all are confronted with the mystery of the glory of God.

Those who are eager for the return of Christ should also be eager to share his good news with the world.

And this gospel of the kingdom will be preached throughout the whole world, as a testimony to all nations; and then the end will come." [Matthew 24:14]

Further Reading

Bloesch, Donald G., *Essentials of Evangelical Theology*, Volume 2. Chapter VII, The Personal Return of Christ, Harper & Row
International Standard Bible Encyclopedia, Vol. 3, article, "Parousia", pp. 664-670
Ladd, George Eldon, *The Blessed Hope*, Eerdmans

Ladd, George Eldon, *Crucial Questions About the Kingdom of God*, Eerdmans

Leitch, Addison H., *Interpreting Basic Theology,* Chapter Thirteen, The Second Advent, Channel Press

For Reflection or Discussion

1. How much attention should Christians give to the second coming of Christ and related truths?

2. Do you think that most Christians overemphasize or underemphasize this doctrine?

3. What practical effect does the teaching regarding the return of Christ have upon you?

CHAPTER NINETEEN
HEAVEN AND ETERNAL LIFE

People belong to the earth--the physical realm--the material universe. It is new birth in Jesus Christ that connects them to the spiritual realm. As one believes in Jesus Christ he is born of the Spirit and his aspirations should more and more be directed toward the realm of God.

> If then you have been raised with Christ, seek the things that are above, where Christ is, seated at the right hand of God. Set your minds on things that are above, not on things that are on earth. [Colossians 3:1,2]

The Bible recognizes and celebrates the vast and impressive physical realm created by God (see, for example, Psalms 19 and 104). But it also affirms that there is a much more marvelous realm which is God's realm--an eternal realm of the spirit--God's dwelling place, which is designated as heaven. Jesus assures us that he will include those who believe in him in his realm.

> Let not your hearts be troubled; believe in God, believe also in me. In my Father's house are many rooms; if it were not so, would I have told you that I go to prepare a place for you? And when I go and prepare a place for you, I will come again and will take you to myself, that where I am you may be also. [John 14:1-3]

In his great chapter on the resurrection, the apostle Paul stated,

> It is sown a physical body, it is raised a spiritual body. If there is a physical body, there is also a spiritual body. Thus it is written, "The first man Adam became a living being"; the last Adam became a life-giving spirit. But it is not the spiritual which is first but the physical, and then the spiritual. The first man was from the earth, a man of dust; the second man is from heaven. As was the man of dust, so are those who are of the dust; and as is the man of heaven, so are those who are of heaven. Just as we have

borne the image of the man of dust, we shall also bear the image of the man of heaven. [I Corinthians 15:44-49]

There is a physical realm. There is also a spiritual realm.

English Bishop, Francis Attebury, wrote,

> Few, without the hope of another life, would think it worth their while to live above the allurements of sense.

Indeed, the first observation that we might make about heaven, is that it gives substance--meaning for this life, and for living this life according to the will of God. Rene Pache wrote in his very fine book, *The Future Life*, "If another world does not exist, nothing in this life makes any sense." All that is wrong will be set right by God. His judgment will come upon those who disregard him, and his blessing upon those who believe in him. Awareness of and belief in the life to come is vital to maintaining the present life in its proper perspective.

We do not know as much about heaven as we might like to know. Our capacities for comprehending that realm are limited. We read in I Corinthians,

> For now we see in a mirror dimly, but then face to face. Now I know in part; then I shall understand fully, even as I have been fully understood. [I Corinthians 13:12]

John wrote,

> Beloved, we are God's children now; it does not yet appear what we shall be, but we know that when he appears we shall be like him, for we shall see him as he is. [I John 3:2]

And again from the apostle Paul,

> because we look not to the things that are seen but to the things that are unseen; for the things that are seen are transient, but the things that are unseen are eternal.
> [II Corinthians 4:18]

We are limited both by our experience and by the capacities of human reason. Perhaps, we are also limited because we are not yet ready for the full disclosure of the heavenly vision just as a three year old is not ready for many of the realities of adulthood.

The idea that we are not yet ready for a clear vision of heaven, is supported by the experience related by the apostle Paul in II Corinthians, chapter 12. He speaks in the third person, but it is evident that he is speaking of himself. He relates that he was caught up to the third heaven, which we believe was a reference to the heaven of God (which he calls paradise). He said that he saw things that it is not lawful for man to utter. Further that because of that experience, in order that he not be too elated (perhaps in order that he return to the reality of this life) he said, a thorn in the flesh was given to him, a messenger of Satan. He asked God three times to deliver him of that thorn. But God assured him that his grace would be sufficient. And Paul bore testimony that in his weakness he had found sufficient strength and power in God. My point is that he had that great experience, which few if any other people have had, but because of it he was given a compensating burden. Perhaps God does not, at this time, reveal more to us about the life to come because we lack the capacity to handle it without experiencing severe psychological or emotional consequences.

We read in the gospels--of Peter, James, and John who went up with Jesus on a mountain. He was transfigured before them. They saw his divine celestial glory. He conversed with Moses and Elijah. There was a cloud, and the voice of God spoke to those who were there, "This is my beloved Son, hear ye him." And what do we read? "They were exceedingly afraid." It was a frightening experience for them. Almost universally in the Bible when the spiritual realm breaks through into the material--when there is an appearance of an angel--there has to be the reassurance, "Fear not!". The opening up of heaven produces fright, even in those who love God and believe in him. John tells of his vision of the glorified risen Christ and he says, "when I saw him I fell at his face as though dead." In his mercy God, undoubtedly, limits our knowledge of the world to come to what is good for us to know. However, much is given to us that we can know and understand. Here are a number of statements that can be made with confidence from the scriptures regarding eternity:

1. <u>Heaven is a holy place</u>. Because God is holy, everything about heaven must be appropriate for the presence of God.

> But nothing unclean shall enter it, nor any one who practices abomination or falsehood, but only those who are written in the Lamb's book of life. [Revelation 21:17]

> But as for the cowardly, the faithless, the polluted, as for murderers, fornicators, sorcerers, idolaters, and all liars, their lot shall be in the lake that burns with fire and brimstone, which is the second death. [Revelation 21:8]

Only goodness, righteousness, truth, and all else that is appropriate to a holy God will be found there.

2. <u>Heaven involves being a new person</u>. The Bible teaches that each of us have a unique identity, and we retain that identity in the life to come. But, as one believes in Jesus Christ, God begins a new work in his life. The believer begins the long journey of progress toward Christlikeness. For many, this process of sanctification may seem both protracted and slow. Nonetheless God begins to change us. We are to grow in the Spirit. We are to become more like Jesus Christ. And that is fulfilled and completed in the life to come. So, that as we shed this body, we are endowed with a spiritual body.

> We know that the whole creation has been groaning in travail together until now; and not only the creation, but we ourselves, who have the first fruits of the Spirit, groan inwardly as we wait for the redemption of our bodies. [Romans 8:22,23]

It is being a new person. What is sown is perishable, what is raised is imperishable.

> But our commonwealth is in heaven, and from it we await a Savior, the Lord Jesus Christ, who will change our lowly body to be like his glorious body, by the power which enables him even to subject all things to himself. [Philippians 3:20,21]

3. <u>The life to come is being like Jesus Christ</u>. We read in

Ephesians, chapter 4,

> until we all attain to the unity of the faith and of the knowledge of the Son of God, to mature manhood, to the measure of the stature of the fulness of Christ;
> [Ephesians 4:13]

> I have been crucified with Christ; it is no longer I who live, but Christ who lives in me; and the life I now live in the flesh I live by faith in the Son of God, who loved me and gave himself for me. [Galatians 2:20]

We are to be like Jesus Christ. And as believers we are to welcome Jesus into our lives. We are to be happy in our relationship with him, because becoming like him is our destiny.

> And we all, with unveiled face, beholding the glory of the Lord, are being changed into his likeness from one degree of glory to another; for this comes from the Lord who is the Spirit. [II Corinthians 3:18]

> Rather, speaking the truth in love, we are to grow up in every way into him who is the head, into Christ,
> [Ephesians 4:15]

4. <u>Heaven is being with God</u>.

> I heard a great voice from the throne saying, "Behold, the dwelling of God is with men. He will dwell with them, and they shall be his people, and God himself will be with them; [Revelation 21:3]

To be in heaven is to be in close association with God, and to know him much more completely and fully that we now know him. Being in the very presence of God and knowing him is of the very essence of heaven. Those who show little interest or inclination to know God now, should ask themselves why they will want to know him in a much fuller sense in the life to come.

5. <u>Additional certainties regarding heaven</u>: Even though our

knowledge is limited, from what we know of God as creator and of his design and of his revealed purposes--we can use our sanctified imaginations to think about the life to come. The Bible tells us that it will mean the absence of sorrow, pain, and death. There will not be any funerals in heaven. There will not be any mourning because there will be neither sickness or dying. There will be no sense of loss; nothing to be sorry about.

If we are to be God's servants in this life, will we not surely continue to be his servants in the life to come? I like the word of the Psalmist who said,

> For a day in thy courts is better than a thousand elsewhere. I would rather be a doorkeeper in the house of my God than dwell in the tents of wickedness. [Psalm 84:10]

To serve the Lord is the highest privilege to which anyone could ever aspire.

There will be majestic music in heaven. Music was integral to the worship of God with the tabernacle and temple. Music continue to be important under the new covenant, and music will be heard in heaven.

> and they sang a new song [Revelation 5:9]

> and they sing a new song before the throne and before the four living creatures and before the elders.
> [Revelation 14:13]

> And they sing the song of Moses, the servant of God, and the song of the Lamb, [Revelation 15:3]

To say the least, the music of heaven will be of an even higher order than the best of the music that we now enjoy!

The scripture says, "Now we see through a glass darkly, then we shall see face to face." Our knowledge will increas immeasurably. God is the greatest scientist. God is the great mathematician.

God is the supreme architect. He is the consummate musician and artist. The expansion of one's knowledge and ability to reason in the life to come will be absolutely incredible.

Surely our senses will be enhanced. What a blessing to enjoy good eyesight, good hearing, and fine senses of small, taste and touch. We are speaking of a congruity with the life to come, but our senses now perceive only a very limited section of the light and sound spectrums. How much greater awareness will we have on a comparable basis in the eternal realm? There will undoubtedly be much greater facility of movement. We remember that the risen Lord, whom we are to resemble, was not restricted by walls and doors. He moved from one place to another without opening doors (to the surprise of the disciples).

How much we enjoy good friendships and relationships in this life. Remove all of the sin and the selfishness and the negatives from this life and we have a hint of how friendships will be enriched in the life to come. Archbishop Whately has an excellent statement on this subject:

> I am convinced that the extension and perfection of friendship will constitute a great part of the future happiness of the blest. Many have lived in various and distant ages and countries, who have been in their characters...in the agreement of their tastes, and suitableness of dispositions, perfectly adapted for friendship with each other, but who of course could never meet in this world. Many a one selects, when he is reading history--a truly pious Christian most especially in reading sacred history--some one or two favorite characters with whom he feels that a personal acquaintance would have been peculiarly delightful to him. Why shoul not such a desire be realized in a future state? A wish to see and personally know, for example, the apostle Paul, or John is the most likely to arise in the noblest and purest mind. I should be sorry to think such a wish absurd and presumptuous, or unlikely ever to be gratified. The highest enjoyment doubtless to the blest will be the personal knowledge of their great and beloved Master. Yet I cannot but think that some part of that happiness will consist in an intimate knowledge of the greatest of his followers also;

Someone asked me, when we are in heaven will we just sit on a cloud playing a harp? Is that all there will be to do in eternity? That and similar questions illustrate the paucity of the knowledge and imagination of many when it comes to contemplating the life to come. When we bring together all of the teachings of the Bible on the subject of heaven--even though we do not see as clearly as we might like--we surely realize that it will indeed be a wonderful, marvelous life. Much fuller, more captivating, and richer than the present.

One of the great experiences of this life is the public worship of God. To adore and praise and honor God brings out the very best in people. How much greater, how much grander, how much more marvelous will be that worship when we are in the very presence of God! Isaac Watts wrote in one of his hymns:

There is a land of pure delight, Where saints immortal reign;
Infinite day excludes the night, And pleasures banish pain.

There everlasting spring abides. And never-withering flowers;
Death, like a narrow sea, divides This heavenly land from ours.

Sweet fields beyond the swelling flood Stand dressed in living green;
So to the Jews old Canaan stood, While Jordan rolled between.

But timorous mortals start and shrink To cross this narrow sea,
And linger shivering on the brink, And fear to launch away.

O could we make our doubts remove, Those gloomy doubts that rise,
And see the Canaan that we love With unbeclouded eyes:

Could we but climb where Moses stood, And view the land scape o'er,
Not Jordan's stream, nor death's cold flood, Should fright us from the shore.

And Robert Montgomery wrote,

If God hath made this world so fair, where sin and death abound, how beautiful, beyond compare, will paradise be found.

These truths regarding the life to come, which are derived from scripture, are neither fantastic nor ephemeral. They speak of the very heart and substance of life. The hope of heaven is to be your hope. It is to be your greatest aspiration.

Further Reading

   Pache, Rene, *The Future Life* Moody Press
   Smith, Wilbur, *The Biblical Doctrine of Heaven,* Moody Press

For Reflection or Discussion

   1. Why is it probably a good thing that our knowledge of the life to come has been restricted?

   2. What is, perhaps, the greatest or most certain characteristic of heaven?

   3. Enumerate a number of characteristics that the Bible associates with heaven.

   4. What keeps Christians from putting a greater emphasis on heaven?

APPENDIX A

NEW TESTAMENT PASSAGES THAT AFFIRM THE DIVINE NATURE OF JESUS CHRIST

Matthew 1:22, 23: "All this took place to fulfill what the Lord had spoken by the prophet: 'Behold, a virgin shall conceive and bear a son, and his name shall be called Emmanuel' (which means, God with us."

Matthew 2:2: "Where is he who has been born king of the Jews? For we have seen his star in the East, and have come to worship him."

Matthew 28:18: "...and going into the house they saw the child with Mary his mother, and they fell down and worshipped him."

Matthew 28:18: "And Jesus came and said to them, 'All authority in heaven and on earth has been given to me. Go therefore and make disciples of all nations, baptizing them in the name of the Father and of the Son and of the Holy Spirit.'"

Mark 2:5-7: "And when Jesus saw their faith, he said to the paralytic, 'My son, your sins are forgiven.' Now some of the scribes were sitting there, questioning in their hearts, 'Why does this man speak thus? It is blasphemy: Who can forgive sins but God alone?'"

Mark 5:6: "And when he saw Jesus from afar, he ran and worshipped him."

Mark 14:61b-64a: "Again the high priest asked him, 'Are you the Christ, the Son of the Blessed?' And Jesus said, 'I am; and you will see the Son of man sitting at the right hand of Power, and coming with the clouds of heaven.' And the high priest tore his mantle, and said, 'Why do we still need witnesses? You have heard his blasphemy ....'"

Luke 5:8: "But when Simon Peter saw it, he fell down at Jesus' knees, saying, 'Depart from me, for I am a sinful man, O Lord.'"

John 1:1-3, 14: "In the beginning was the Word, and the Word was with God, and the Word was God. He was in the beginning with God; all things were made through him, and without him was not anything made that was made .... And the Word became flesh and dwelt among us, full of grace and truth and we have beheld his glory, glory as of the only Son from the Father."

John 5:17,18: "But Jesus answered them, 'My Father is working still, and I am working.' This was why the Jews sought all the more to kill him, because he not only broke the sabbath but also called God his Father making himself equal with God."

John 8:42: "Jesus said to them, 'If God were your Father, you would love me, for I proceeded and came forth from God; I came not of my own accord, but he sent me.'"

John 8:58-59: "Jesus said to them, 'Truly, truly, I say to you, before Abraham was, I am.' So they took up stones to throw at him; but Jesus hid himself, and went out of the temple."

John 10:30: "I and the Father are one."

John 10:37-8: "If I am not doing the works of my Father, then do not believe me; but if I do them, even though you do not believe me, believe the works, that you may know and understand that the Father is in me and I am in the Father."

John 14:8-11: "Philip said to him, 'Lord show us the Father, and we shall be satisfied.' Jesus said to him, 'Have I been with you so long, and yet you do not know me, Philip? He who has seen me has seen the Father; how can you say, Show us the Father? Do you not believe that I am in the Father and the Father in me? The words that I say to you I do not speak on my own authority, but the Father who dwells in me does his works. Believe me that I am in the Father and the Father in me; or else believe me for the sake of the works themselves.'"

John 17:5: "... and now, Father, glorify thou me in thy own presence with the glory which I had with thee before the world was made...."

John 20:28: "Thomas answered him, 'My Lord and my God!'"

I Corinthians 8:6: "... yet for us there is one God, the Father; from whom are all things and for whom we exist, and one Lord, Jesus Christ, through whom are all things and through whom we exist."

II Corinthians 4:4: "In their case the god of this world has blinded the minds of the unbelievers, to keep them from seeing the light of the gospel of the glory of Christ, who is the likeness of God."

II Corinthians 5:19a: "... that is, God was in Christ reconciling the world to himself ... "

II Corinthias 13:14: "The grace of the Lord Jesus Christ and the love of God and the fellowship of the Holy Spirit be with you all."

Philippians 2:5-7: "Have this mind among yourselves, which you have in Christ Jesus,, who, though he was in the form of God, did not count equality with God a thing to be grasped, but emptied himself, taking the form of a servant, being born in the likeness of men."

Philippians 2:9-11: "Therefore God has highly exalted him and bestowed on him the name which is above every name, that at the name of Jesus every knee should bow, in heaven and on earth and under the earth, and every tongue confess that Jesus Christ is Lord, to the glory of God the Father."

Colossians 1:15: "He is the image of the invisible God, the first-born of all creation."

Colossians 1:18-19: "He is the head of the body, the church; he is the beginning, the first-born from the dead, that in everything he mgiht be pre-eminent. For in him all the fulness of God was pleased to dwell ..."

Colossians 1:15: "For in him the whole fulness of deity dwells bodily …"

I Timothy 2:3: "This is good, and it is acceptable in the sight of God our Saviour …"

Titus 1:3,4: "… and at the proper time manifested in this word through the preaching with which I have been entrusted by command of God our Saviour; to Titus, my true child in a common faith: Grace and peace from God the Father and Christ Jesus our Savior."

Titus 2:13: "… awaiting our bless hope, the appearing of the glory of our great God and Savior Jesus Christ …"

Titus 3:4,6: "… but when the goodness and lovingkindness of God our Savior appears, … which he poured out upon us richly through Jesus Christ our Savior …"

Hebrews 1:2,3a: "… but in these last days he has spoken to us by as Son, whom he appointed the heir of all things, through whom also he created the world. He reflects the glory of God and bears the very stamp of his nature, upholding the universe by his word and power."

Hebrews 1:5,6: "For to what angel did God ever say, 'Thou art my Son, today I have begotten thee?' Or again, 'I will be to him a father, and he shall be to me a son?' And again, when he rings the firstborn into the world, he says, 'Let all God's angels worship.'"

II John 9: "Any one who goes ahead and does not abide in the doctrine of Christ does not have God; he who abides in the doctrine has both the Father and the Son."

Jude 24, 25: "Now to him who is able to keep you from falling and to present you without blemish before the presence of his glory with rejoicing, to the only God, our Savior thorugh Jesus Christ our Lord, be glory, majesty, dominion, and authority, before all time and now and forever. Amen."

INDEX

Aaron 52
Abortion 44, 167, 174
Abraham 21, 28, 29, 42, 51, 109,
            136-139, 141, 156, 161
Adam and Eve 34-37, 45-47, 137
Adler, Mortimer 75
Agrippa, king 136
Ahab 173
AIDS 118
American Standard Version 1
A-millenial 185
Angel 78, 114
Animism 8
Antioch 81, 99
Antichrist 182
Antinomianism 69, 72
Apostle's Creed 56
Armenians 43
Ascension 178
Assyria 53
Attebury, Francis 188
Authority of Jesus
    Christ 115-126, 161, 166, 167

Baal 18
Babylon 53
Baptism 71, 149
Barnabas 90, 94
Beroea 5
Bhuddism 8, 9
Bolivia 43
Born Again 89, 90
Boswell 80
Buckley, William 117
Burke, Edmund 10

Caanan 28, 137, 173
Caesarea 55, 99
California 44, 159
Calvin, John 5, 31, 84, 85
Cambodia 43
Carter, Jimmy 89
Chambers, Whittaker 40
Child Battering 44
Church 5, 45, 66, 86, 96,
            121, 122, 127-134, 157-167, 174
Civil War, American 43

Clean and Unclean Foods 3
Colson, Charles 66, 124, 125
Columbus, Christopher 158, 159
Communion Service 54, 65
Conner, Dennis 116, 117
Constitution
    of the U.S. 117
Corinth 45, 81
Cornelius 92, 99
Cosmic Signs 181
Cosmology 14, 15
Covenant 24, 53, 55, 68, 85, 108-
            110, 135-146, 175, 192
Creation 5, 6, 15, 122-125,
            141, 187, 192
Creationism 6
Creeds 4
Cross of Christ 69, 129, 145, 176
Crucifixion 76, 77, 83, 98
Crusades 130

Day of Atonement 139
Damascus 99, 136
Daniel 120, 182
David 85, 108, 119, 120, 184
Deacons 90, 98, 99, 130
Death 192, 194
Devil 41-50, 185
Drugs 43, 82

Ecclesiology 85
Egypt 17, 18, 51, 137
Elder 130
Elijah 18, 103, 173, 189
Emerging Trends 9
Ephesus 81, 92
Eternal Life 187-196
Eternity 16, 17, 194
Evangelism 156-165, 167

Faith 49, 63, 70, 71, 100, 101,
            104, 113, 145, 147
Felix 55
Flood 6
Forgiveness 90, 102, 147, 162
Franciscan Friars 159

201

Galilee, Sea of 13
Gallup Surveys 41
Gethsemane........................ 76, 98
Gifts of the Spirit 95
Godfearers.................................. 54
God Is Light 6
Gog and Magog 185
Good Samaritan.................. 168, 169
Greeks.. 53
Green, Michael......................... 145
Greenleaf, Simon 77

Hagar 28
Hawaii....................................... 66
Heaven 75, 111, 183-185, 187-196
Hedonism 8
Heidelberg Catechism 57
Hell... 41
Henry II (England) 107
Herod Antipas 76
High Priest 68, 139, 141
Hinduism.................................... 8
Hodge, Charles 55
Holocost..................................... 43
Holy of Holies 139
Holy Place 139
Holy Spirit 2, 4, 26, 83, 85-96, 98, 111, 141, 148, 149, 155, 158, 187, 190

Individualism 5
Inspiration of Scripture 1-11
Iran 43
Iraq 43
Isaac.................. 51, 75, 109, 139, 141
Isaiah 2, 3, 13, 24, 42, 153, 178
Ishmael...................................... 28
Islam...................................... 8, 132

Jacob 109, 139, 141
James (disciple)................ 13, 101, 189
Jehovah's Witnesses.................... 123
Jeremiah................................... 136
Jerusalem 76, 81, 91, 92, 98, 103, 121, 136, 157, 160, 178, 181
Jezebel 174
Job......................... 12, 13, 47, 50
John 13, 78, 92, 101, 124, 189
Johnson, Samuel 80
John the Baptist........................ 111
Jonah 23, 24, 74, 109

Joseph of Arimathea 73
Joshua...................................... 173
Judas................................... 47, 98
Jubilee, year of 173
Judgment 51-61-69, 176
Justice 166-177

Kingdom of God .. 19, 56, 87, 91, 107-114, 119, 130, 177, 184, 185
King James Version 1
Korea 163

Ladd, George Eldon 81
Latourette, Kenneth Scott............ 132
Lebanon 116
Leitch, Addison 33, 35
Levi... 52
Lewis, C.S. 40
Lord's Prayer, the 102, 105, 113
Lot 137
Love 61, 67, 96, 132, 151, 162
Luther, Martin 5, 70, 85, 124

Macedonia 63, 64
Manna 18
Mary Magdeline 78
Mary, mother of Jesus 140, 178
Marxism................................... 8, 9
Mayer, Milton 33
McFarland, Robert 171
Messiah 73, 91, 92, 119, 120, 123, 175, 178, 183, 184
Milennium................................ 183
Mill, John Stuart 150, 151
Moses 12, 13, 15, 21, 42, 52, 55, 75, 109, 136, 138, 140, 189
Muggeridge, Malcolm 66

Naboth 173, 174
New Birth 147-155, 187
New English Bible............................ 1
New Internatonal Version............... 1
Nicene Creed.............................. 56
Nicodemus 21, 73, 87, 148
Niebuhr, Reinhold 40, 66
Nineveh 23, 24
Nixon, Richard..................... 124, 125
Noah 137
North, Oliver........................... 171

Omnipotence......................... 16, 17
Omnipresence........................ 16, 17
Omniscience.......................... 16, 17

Pache, Rene 188
Palm Sunday 178
Pantheism 75
Paul, apostle 5, 6, 47, 54, 63, 64,
79, 88, 90, 99, 105,
121, 129, 136, 149,
152, 179, 187-189
Peace 174-177
Pentecost 86, 91, 92, 98, 129,
153, 157, 160
Pentecostal 86, 92
Persia 53
Peter, Simon .. 8, 13, 14, 44, 47, 78-80,
92, 94, 99, 101-103,
124, 153, 189
Pharaoh 15
Pharisee 21, 27, 79, 97
Philippi 63, 99
Philistines 85, 108
Pilate 53, 54, 73, 76, 77
Planned Parenthood 117
Playboy Magazine 8
Poindexter, Admiral 171
Pope 5
Pope Alexander VI 159
Post-milennial 184
Pre-milennial 184
Prayer 19, 49, 97-106,
154, 163, 177
Prodigal Son 27, 28
Property Rights 172, 173
Protestant Reformation 4, 85, 86,
130, 158

Qumran 2

Rapture 180
Resurrection 18, 73-84, 187
Return of Christ 119, 131, 133,
177, 178-186
Righteousness 69, 166-177
Rimirez, Richard 43
Rome, Romans 53-55, 81, 103, 142
Russia For Christ 82

Sabbath 139
Sacraments 86
Salvation 1, 63-71, 124, 127,
147, 149
Samaria 92
Samson 85
Samuel 108, 116
Sanctification 2, 97, 147-155, 189

Sanhedrin 73
San Salvador 159
Sarah 51, 137
Satan 12, 34, 35, 41-50,
182, 185, 189
Saul, king 85, 108, 116
Savings and Loan Crisis 44
Scientism 8
Scots Confession 56
Sheen, Fulton J. 70
Silas 63, 64
Sin 32, 64, 70, 102, 147
Sinai 12, 52, 53, 137, 138
Sodom and Gomorrah 51
Solar System 14
Solzhenitsyn, Alexander 66
Sotierology 85
Soviet Union 82
Spurgeon, Charles H. 104
Stephen 80, 94, 99
Synagogue 54, 129

Tabernacle 52, 68, 139
Television 171
Temple 68, 74, 139
Temptation 48, 97
Ten Commandments 52, 65,137,
138, 143
Thielicke, Helmut 66
Thomas 79
Thompson, Francis 22
Tongues 93
Tolkien, J.R.R 68
Tozer, A.W. 97
Transcendence of God 7, 75
Tribulation 180, 181
Truth 48, 112, 171, 176

United States 43, 44, 113
Universe 14
Uzziah 13

Viet Nam 43

Watergate 171
Watts, Isaac 194
Whately, archbishop 193
World Mission 156-165, 167
Worship 194

Zacchaeus 168
Zwingli 5

203